SM(

Ur
NORTH AMERICA

A Journey of Discovery

Second Edition
Illustrated

M. R. Ross

MultiCultural Educational
Publishing Company

MultiCultural Educational Publishing Company
PO Box 1054, Jerome, AZ 86331
(928) 649-5449
E-mail: orders@mcepub.com

First Printing October 2006

10 9 8 7 6 5 4 3 2

ISBN 0-9703721-3-2

Illustrations by Ron Dilg

Disclaimer: Many of the smoke plants in this book were used in historic times by indigenous herbal practitioners. Complete information on these smoke plants and their use is not available. The information that is available is presented in this book for historical and educational purposes only. The Publisher and the Author do not recommend the smoking or use of these plants by the reader. The Author and Publisher shall be held blameless for any injury to the reader that may occur from the smoking or ingestion of any of these plants.

Dedicated—

To the places I have lived.

Indian Tobacco (*Lobelia infata*)

Contents

LIST OF ILLUSTRATIONS

Acknowledgments

I want to thank E.J.Young for introducing me to smoke plants, and my friends and teachers in Tahlequah, Cherokee Nation, especially Dawn Caldwell (Sauk and Fox/Quapaw), for helping me learn about Native American history and culture from the inside. I thank my sister, Julia Ross, for her encouragement and astute editing wisdom which transformed this book. I thank my friends, Christina Sandoval and Linda Kuschel, for sharing my exploration of smoking a different kind of plant and Deborah Ultan for her inspiring spirit. Thanks to Jamie Moffett for giving me the kind of support I've always dreamed of (*especially* with PageMaker); to Jeanna Napoleon for her enthusiasm; and to Erich Schienke for his brilliant critique. My deepest thanks to the trees and plants of Tahlequah and the "plant people" of the Mountain and the Gulch for their wisdom and healing.

Preface

My journey of discovery of smoke plants was an unplanned adventure into unknown territory. When I began to write a "little" book about my personal experience, I expected to find about a dozen smoke plants to share. I was amazed to discover over 150. However, there is much more to be learned about smoke plants than is contained in this book. There is a great deal of ethnobotanical information that I have not researched. There are clinical applications for herbalists to explore, especially in the areas of mental and nervous illnesses. There also exists vast knowledge of smoke plants held by the elders and herbalists of the Navajo/Diné, Cherokee, Lakota, Iroquois, Hopi and other Native Americans. Through their traditions, they have access to a deeper knowledge of smoke and its healing and spiritual properties than can be transmitted through the written word.

I want to thank those herbalists, healers, elders, ethnobotanists, and friends, past and present, from the Western European and Native American traditions, who have shared their knowledge about plants so that I and others may learn from them.

Jerome, Arizona
August, 2002

Fennel (*Foeniculum vulgare*)

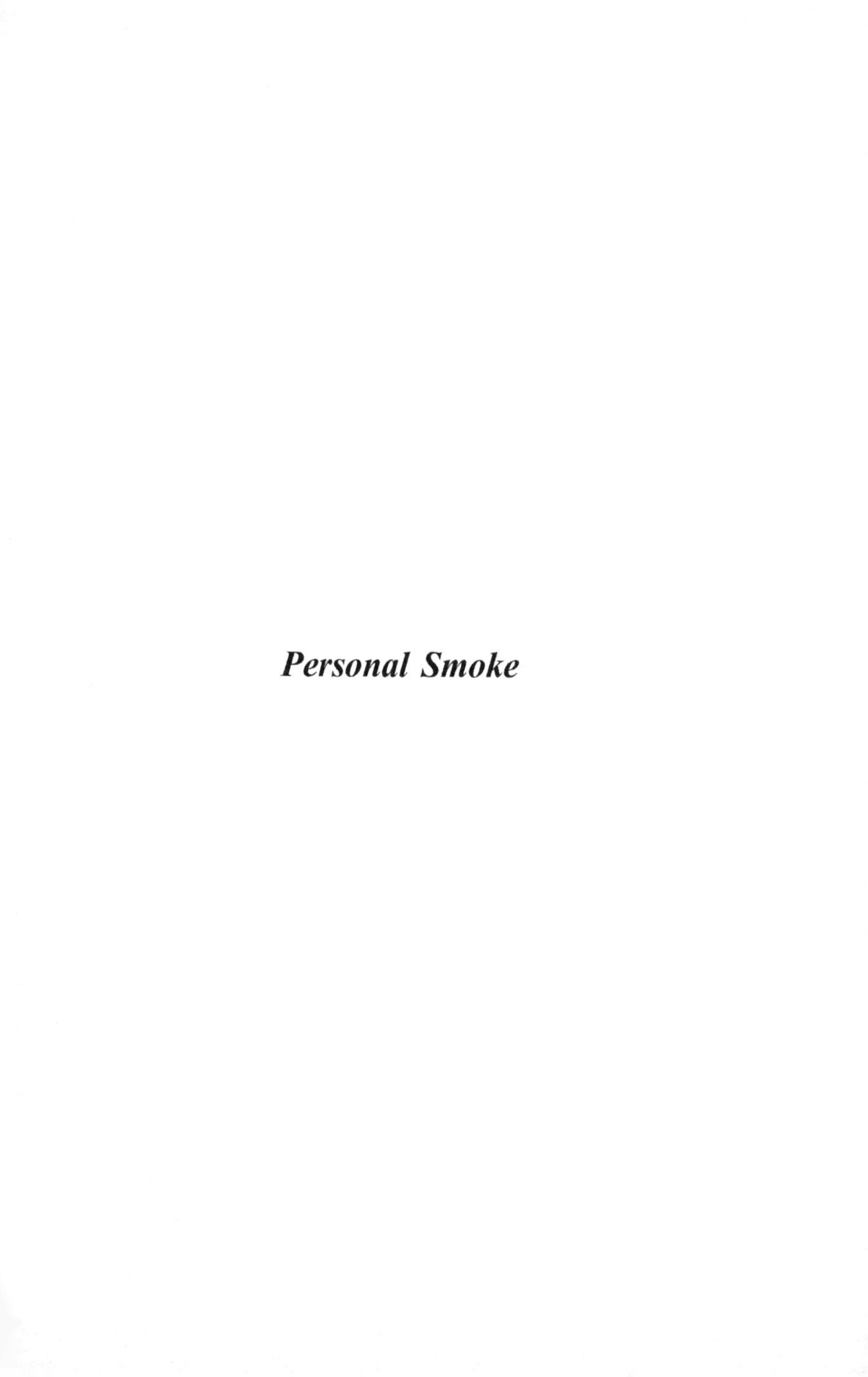

Personal Smoke

Your life is your breath.

Smoke is breath made visible.

When we smoke together,
our breaths are carried by the plant's energy
and visibly joined as one.

The energy of every plant is different.
I have a special interest in plants
that help the nervous system.
My nervous system collapsed at one time,
so that is the path I was given.
I spent a year healing
inTahlequah, Cherokee Nation,
and that is where I learned about
the power of smoke.

Smoking plants had an immediate calming
effect upon my nervous system. They were a gift.

Personal plants are plants given to you—
by other people and by Nature itself.
They carry the power of the plant
and the power of the giver.
My smoke mix is from
plants that were given to me.

Spinning Coyote Smoke Mix

Damiana—a sweet-smelling, gentle nervine. Helps keep the heart open during difficult times.

Mullein—helps soothe inflamed lungs. It is the base of many smoke mixes. It is a very gentle herb and has no known toxic effect.

Passionflower— soothes the mind. A nervine and a sedative, it is especially helpful for nerves that have been stressed by worrying and overthinking.

Manzanita—one of the most frequently used herbs in smoke mixes by First Nation people. It's an astringent, grounding element in a smoke mix.

Skullcap— relaxes rigid muscles. Helps stop obsessive thinking and grounds the mind in the body. Good for insomnia.

Fennel (or anise) seed—a wonderful aroma, lifts the heart.

Tahlequah, Cherokee Nation—When I was living in Tahlequah, my friend Dawn Caldwell (Sauk & Fox/Quapaw) gave me a copy of a Cheyenne story titled *Coyote Who Wanted to Dance with the Stars*. Dawn is a scholar of Native American Studies who grew up dancing on PowWow Highway, the partly mythical, mostly real string of PowWows that winds through Indian Country. I learned a lot from her generous sharing of Indian Way.

The way I remember the story is:

> Coyote sat down on Earth and watched the stars spinning across the night sky. He wanted to be up high with the stars, spinning and dancing. So Coyote flew up to the stars, spinning across the sky higher and higher, faster and faster, until he went so fast that his arms and legs flew off and he crashed to the ground. Coyote's desire for that high, fast, spinning star dance was so great he didn't learn the first time he crashed, or the second time. The third time he went so fast, and so high, that his head flew off, all his arms and legs fell off, and his whole body flew to pieces and he was scattered all over the Earth. It took him a long, long time to find all the pieces of himself and put himself back together again.

I didn't get it the first time I read it. About a week later, it hit me. This was my story. I think this is the story for a lot of us.When we want to be something we aren't, when we go too fast, too high, try to achieve an ideal life, or an ideal relationship, or an ideal career that is humanly impossible, sooner or later our bodies fall apart, our identities crash, and it takes a long time to find all the pieces and put ourselves back together.

That's why sometimes I think of my smoke mix as the Spinning Coyote Smoke Mix. It reminds me to slow down and enjoy myself as a mere mortal here on Earth.

Damiana—the innocent heart

Mexico—I lived in a palm-thatched bungalow at the mouth of the biggest arroyo in Baja California, Sur. When it flooded, the water rushed down from storms in the mountains and emptied into the ocean, leaving behind mounds of ancient cardon and cholla wood, which I gathered and used for special fires.

The sun rose from behind a snag-toothed mountain and shone with bright radiance through the windows into the house each morning. Two tall coconut palm trees stood on either side of the house, which had blue windows, the color of the sky. Hummingbirds raced through the garden.

One day my closest neighbor and friend, Cruz, who was in her early twenties, came to visit. She had been born in the *huerta*, the farms near the ocean, married an American surfer twenty-five years her senior when she was eighteen, and traveled the world, moving into a completely new reality with an instinctual dignity and poise.

She held out a paper bag filled with scraggly, twiggy plant. It was Damiana. I didn't think it looked like much.

"This is for you," she said. "For the woman problem. It's good for lovemaking, too," she added, raising her eyebrows and giving me a mischievous glance.

Her aunt is a known *curandera* in Pescadero. She had asked her aunt for a plant that would help with some hormonal imbalances I was having.

Cruz had great courage, great heart, great love, great playfulness. Many early mornings, we sat on the beach in front of her house, watching our men surf, while her red-headed son, Alejandro, played in the sand beside us. After surfing, she would make us strong, hot coffee to drink.

Gift properties—gently opens sexual channels, keeps the heart open.

Mullein—the scholar/warrior

Tahlequah, Cherokee Nation—The weather was sweltering, high humidity, high heat, as I walked down the main street of Tahlequah, Oklahoma, in August. I saw the flyer stuck on the window of one of the stores. A class in Cherokee history would be taught at the courthouse. It would be the first community class on Cherokee history sponsored by the Cherokee Nation. A brilliant young Cherokee professor would teach it with impeccable historical accuracy. A group of us started meeting at E.J.'s little cabin after class to talk about Cherokee history, culture, good books and local gossip.

I watched him take the pipe out of his deerskin pouch, slowly and calmly break up the herbs, slowly and calmly fill the pipe, and puff gentle, aromatic smoke into the air and my ragged nerves edged down a notch, or two, just watching.

We went looking for Mullein outside of town and found it at one of the family cemeteries. There was a plant or two in his yard as well.

He told me of his time in Vietnam. He was a captain on the border of Cambodia. There was a lot of action there. He made a vow to bring all of his men back alive and he kept that vow. He said that his smoke mix had helped him a lot in dealing with the residue of Agent Orange problems and Post Traumatic Stress Syndrome.

His great-grandfather, who had been a judge of the Cherokee Nation during Allotment, stood in the front row of a group photograph that hung on the Cherokee Nation courthouse wall. He looked just like him.

When I left town, he gave me a deerskin pouch he had stitched, a clay pipe with Otter sculpted by Cherokee artist Murv Jacob, a knife with an eagle etched on it, a lighter in a snakeskin cover, some pipe cleaners and screens, and a bag of his smoke mix. Some of the herbs were from South Carolina Cherokee land, and some were from Tahlequah. After I got to Arizona, I sent him some Manzanita.

Gift properties—restores spirit with gentleness and generosity, clears the lungs, restores the breath.

Passionflower— the master herbalist

Bisbee, Arizona—Linda, a friend in Mexico, had moved up to the States. She was investigating schools of herbalism and one of them was in Bisbee, Arizona. She invited me to accompany her on an exploration tour of Arizona, including checking out the school in Bisbee. We met at the Phoenix airport and rented a car. When we got to Bisbee, a quaint old mining town in southern Arizona, we tried to call the school, but no one answered. We asked around the small town, but no one seemed to have heard of it or know where it was, even though we had read that it was world-famous and sometimes it took years to get a place in the school. We drove up and down the main highway, looking for a sign. Finally, we went to a cactus garden outside of town and the man there gave us directions.

It was a modest, one-story building with a lot of cars parked out front. When we walked up, the students were taking a break. They were friendly and invited us in. The administrator, Donna, invited us to stay for the class, held in one room with about 30 students sitting at long tables.

Michael Moore entered the room and heaved his rotund body into a chair. The class was on Passion-flower. He spoke of it with great intelligence, warmth, wisdom and humor. He had used it in free clinics in the sixties to bring hippies down from bad drug trips. Good for the nerves, especially overwired ones. He passed around a bottle of tincture. I'd never seen tinctures before. It was the herb soaked in alcohol, then drained, then squirted into your mouth. Michael is one of those brilliant old hippies who saved first-hand herbal practice from disappearing completely from the Western knowledge reservoir.

When I returned to Oklahoma, I researched Passionflower. A book by the Rodale Press said you could smoke it. My sister said she'd seen it growing around town. I walked along the roads outside of Tahlequah looking for it. I found one beautiful, exotic looking, purple flower on a vine. Passsionflower.

Gift properties—Esoteric knowledge, wisdom, calms the mind.

Manzanita—from the mountain

Verde Valley, Arizona—I moved in with Linda on a ranch she was caretaking near Camp Verde, Arizona, that sat right at the base of a mountain. My private name for it was Avatar Peak. It marked the exact geographic center of Arizona. Every morning that I walked out and saw that mountain, it gave me great hope that one day I would recover. It was a great healing presence in my life. I made up poems and songs to it.

Avatar Mountain, Avatar Peak
Help me find what it is I seek.
Help me find peace of mind,
Help me have a heart that's kind.

For the first few months, all we did was collect rocks. We hiked for hours on the mountain, filling our packs, our pockets, the back of her truck with red agate, creamy jasper, petrified wood, quartz, hematite, granite, salt crystals, geodes, and more. We built a seven-ring labyrinth with the rocks in the space between the house and the pond. After the rock frenzy and the completion of the labyrinth, we started looking at the plants.

My friend in Tahlequah had asked me to send him some Manzanita, so I was on the lookout for that. It was several months before I found it. I was walking by myself, off any trail, my eyes scanning the hundreds of agates that lay on the ground and I almost ran into a thicket of Manzanita. The branches were strong and smooth, burnished a deep, bright red. Its wood felt like hard muscle under satiny skin. It had leathery, green leaves. Amidst the withdrawn, dry winter energy of the desert plants surrounding it, Manzanita's dynamic life-force burst out in a radiating force field. It felt indestructible. Beautiful and indestructible. I later learned it is called "the Phoenix plant." Not even fire can destroy Manzanita. I broke off a branch and hung it upside down on the chest of drawers in my room. After it dried, I sent some to E.J. in Tahlequah.

Gift properties—indestructible life force, the Thunderbird or Phoenix energy that rises from the ashes, recovery from great loss.

Skullcap—teacher of body and breath

Jerome, Arizona—I knew I was too much in my head. Too much worry, too much thinking, too much future and past and not enough present. I had asked Spirit for help. I met Jamie the day I moved to Jerome, an old mining town on the side of a mountain. On my drive up the mountain that day, a brilliant double rainbow arched across the apex of the sky. He taught me Five Element Qigong— five easy and gentle movements that I could do every day that connected the five main energy organ systems of my body. I did them while my coffee was brewing. Qigong means connecting breath (qi or chi) and movement (gong)—breath and body. Grounding Spirit on Earth.

He took me hiking to ancient Indian ruins not on any map. We sat on the ridge that separated two valleys, our backs against the sun-warmed stone walls, and ate smoked salmon sandwiches.

When we ate at his house, he fed me apricot jam and blackberry jam and peach jam that he had made from fruits on his land. He let me lick the spoon.

On Easter, we hiked to a waterfall and pool in a desert canyon. We watched two long, slender, striped snakes glide into the water and swim.

I showed him a picture of Skullcap. "I think I've seen it. I think it grows here in the Gulch," he said. "We'll look for it this summer when it flowers."

Gift Properties—Grounds the mind in the Earth energies, relaxes rigid muscles, opens the body to new ways.

Fennel—gathering sweetness

Deception Gulch, Arizona—It was the first warm day of Spring. Jamie and I took off our shoes and sat in his front yard, letting the sun beat down hot on our skin. In the distance, across the valley, we could see the cliffs of Sedona, layered with bands of red, orange and gold. I picked a little at the grass around my bare feet.

"Look," I said. "There's Mint here!" And next to the Mint were some tiny Horehound leaves just sprouting out of the earth, and next to them were baby Clover leaves. Fennel pushed up its hardy stems a few feet away. I picked a miniature bouquet of Mint, Horehound, Fennel and Clover and popped it in my mouth, delighting in the sweet juices.

The old Fennel stalks stood at the edge of the yard. There were still some seeds left by the birds.

"I could smoke these Fennel seeds instead of the Anise I've been buying," I said to Jamie, and went into the house for a plastic bag. I came back and started gathering the seeds.

Gift Properties—a little sweetness that lifts the heart.

"...I can tell you about my own medicines. I do not know about other people's medicines nor their uses of the same plant."

An individual of the Midewiwin,
a Chippewa healing society
How Indians Use Wild Plants for Food, Medicine & Crafts, p. 323
Frances Densmore

Passionflower (*Passiflora incarnata*)

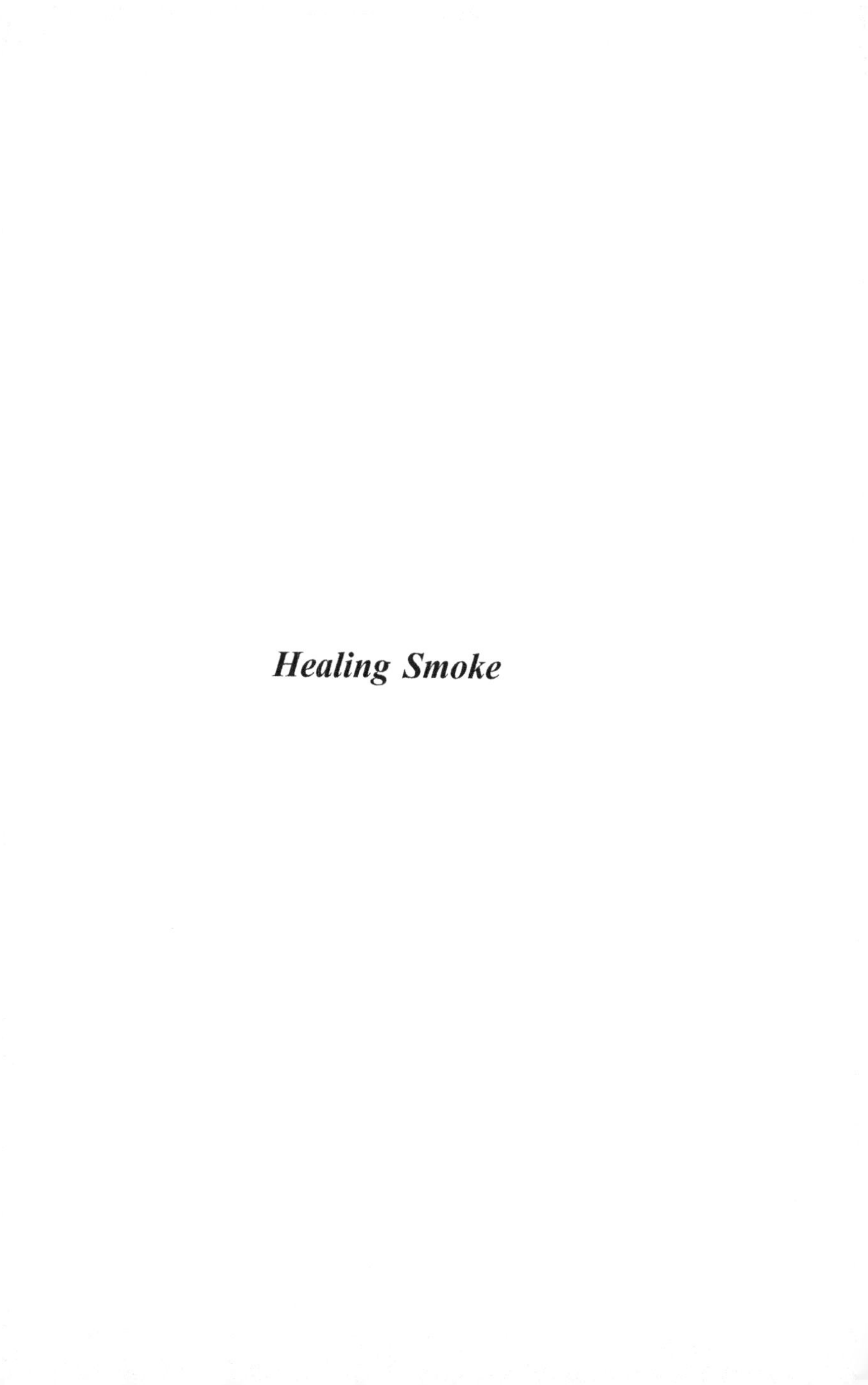

Healing Smoke

Plants that are smoked have the power
to transform the mind very quickly.

The Navajo have a highly developed
use of plants for smoke medicine
and refer to all of these plants as "tobacco."
There is documention of over 50 plants
used by the Navajo as "tobacco."

Joseph Winter
Tobacco Use by Native
North Americans,
Sacred Smoke and Silent Killer
pp. 274-275

"Medicine plants provide
physical cleansing and healing
while tobaccos heal the mind…
Diné tobaccos are called *hozhooji nat'oh*
or Beauty Way tobaccos.
They are used for prayer and meditation
and to strengthen the mind."

Cimi Boone, Irie Herbs flyer
*Traditional Diné Herbs for
the Healing of the Nations*

"In an account of a Seneca council assembly in 1669, it was noted that the Senecas say that good thoughts come from smoking."

Joseph D. McGuire
"Pipes and Smoking Customs of the American Aborigenes,
Based on Material in the U.S. National Museum"
Annual Report of the Smithsonian Institution, 1897 I:550.

"Pipe smokers tend to be introverts with a high
degree of wakefulness and arousal,
so high in fact that ritualistic puffing
on the tobacco pipe calms them
and renders their lives more efficient
and comfortable."

J.P. Beaumier & L. Camp
The Pipe Smoker, p. 40

"The plants—[they have] to be
categorized into two groups.
Healing a physical phase of human ailment,
and then the second part I would
classify as a pyschological healing...
and it mostly focuses around smokes.
They're the emphasis in that category."

Jerome Jackson, Navajo Plant Gatherer
Official Journal of the Arizona Ethnobotanical Research Association
Vol. 2, No. 1, p.8
Fall Equinox, 2000

Nerve Storm

Tahlequah, Cherokee Nation—It was a mild winter, crisply cold but good walking weather. It had been a year since I arrived and my nerves were greatly improved. I was well enough to take a couple of classes at the university. Nothing too stressful. My life had settled into a routine of university classes, research, Cherokee history class, and a daily walk across campus down to the spring that bubbled up under the Bald Cypresses and Sycamores.

I had made friends with E.J. at Cherokee history class and he lived only a few blocks from me in a little cabin that a friend of my sister's had built. Even though it was in the middle of town, it felt like it was in the country. My sister had once lived there and helped register the property as a Pocket Nature Preserve with the State of Oklahoma. That way, they didn't have to mow the lawn. A little stream ran along the side of the property and dozens of varieties of plants grew in a wild, weedy array.

It was hard to know what would trigger a nerve storm, but a bad one hit one day as I was walking down to the spring. My mind freaked and got stuck on some past trauma and my nervous system entered the pain zone. The feeling was somewhat like having a dentist's drill going in your brain for hours that ever once in awhile strikes an open nerve. I took

St. John's Wort and that helped. Kind of like novacaine.

I decided to go visit E.J. hoping that would distract me until the storm subsided.

He had fixed up the small living room with a long work table. On it were boxes filled with deer antler, leather pieces, beads, wire, tools and other craft materials. A nice piece of deerskin hung on the ladder back of a wooden kitchen chair. An old wicker chair with faded, soft cushions sat under a good reading lamp and a wooden carving of a snake squatted on the upstairs landing. It was a gray day, so the lamp was on and spread a warm glow in the room.

E.J. sat me down in the wicker chair and we started talking about something, I don't remember what. He sat over by the table and started fiddling with his pipe and his pouch. He had one pipe of red clay sculpted in the shape of Bear holding the bowl. He had another one made of antler with a reed stem wrapped in leather and tiny beads. He pulled some herbs out of his pouch and started breaking them up and tamping them into the bowl of the Bear pipe.

"What are you smoking?" I asked. I had seen him smoke his pipe at our get-togethers after Cherokee history class, but had never asked him about it.

"Oh a little Mullein, a little Sage, some Uva Ursi, Deer's Tongue, a little of this a little of that."

I had never heard of any of those plants in my life, except maybe Sage. And I certainly had never heard of *smoking* them. I watched him light the pipe, take a few puffs, lean back, relax. It was mesmerizing – watching the curl of the smoke and smelling the herbs.

"Can I try it?" I asked boldly, ignoring my shrieking nerves.

I had never been a smoker, but I was drawn to these pipes and this smoke. But I was anxious, too. What were these herbs? Would I get high? Were they legal? Were they addictive? Did E.J. know what he was doing? Was it possible that they could be poisonous, or make me sick?

"Sure," he said, handing me the pipe.

I was very awkward, fumbling with his Zippo lighter so much that he finally had to light the pipe for me. I puffed a few short puffs, then a long one, then a few more. I sat back in the chair with the pipe in my hand and I felt better. My nerve storm was over. Just like that. The mental pain was gone.

Manzanita (*Arctostaphylos* sp.)

Sharing Smoke

"The relationship between plants and people...
is the source of life."

Jerome Jackson, Navajo Plant Gatherer
Official Journal of the Arizona Ethnobotanical Research Association
Vol. 2, No. 1, p.5
Fall Equinox, 2000

Smoke was traditionally used in North American
First Nation rituals to connect people
together in a sacred space.
An agreement made with smoke
was considered a deeply binding agreement.
It's as if smoking with someone
binds our spirit with theirs.
That is why I really don't want to be
in a smoke-filled room with a lot of strangers.

"As the Sacred Pipes went around the circle,
the smoke from each flowed together
and became one offering, and the people
became one, voicing one prayer."

Jordan Paper
World Council of Churches, 1987
Native Leaders of Central
British Columbia
Offering Smoke, p. 114

"Sometimes an old man and his wife smoked a little
before going to bed, and old men might smoke
when gathered in the dance house
listening to someone tell stories."

George Foster
A Summary of Yuki Culture
quoted in "The Sacred Use of Tobacco"
Elain Cimino, Ann Marie Sayers and
Richard Roods
Costanoan Ohlone Indian Canyon
Resource Web site

Linda

Verde Valley, Arizona—Linda and I drifted out to the pond, usually in the late afternoon or right around sunset, for a smoke. I had given her a Rabbit pipe from Tahlequah. She glued turquoise chips in its eyes.

Worried that she might crack the clay bowl by knocking out the ashes, she strung some beads together and at the end of the string she tied a little piece of coral that she'd collected from one of her ocean dives. She tied the string of beads onto the pipe stem so she always had something to dig out the ashes with. She made one for me with rose quartz, crystal, and hematite beads that she'd carried around with her since the sixties. It looked gorgeous, and that little piece of coral was a good tool, too.

The pond was ringed with a wild tangle of huge old Cottonwoods, Mesquite, Yellow Evening Primrose, Blue Witch, Horehound, Cat's Claw, Tumbleweed, Orange Globe Mallow, Buffalo Gourd, and unidentified weeds. From the dock, we looked up at the mountain peak and the mesas and mountain ranges that surrounded Verde Valley. The Verde River was just on the other side of the corn field. The resident blue herons sometimes flew past in silent grandeur and packs of coyotes howled nearby. When I thought of the people who had lived in this paradise not that long ago, and their forced removal from this land, the pain of loss and grief gripped my heart.

We sat on the steps of the concrete slab right next to the water, sometimes out on the wooden dock, and sometimes we'd take the kayaks out on the pond, and smoke, letting our worries drift away, dissolving into the light.

Christina

Del Mar, California—I'd spent the weekend in San Diego, visiting my best friend, and was preparing for the eight-hour drive back to Arizona. It was the usual, slightly frenzied running around, packing, getting-ready-to-go energy, the adrenalin starting to surge, my mind already on the freeway.

We hugged and then I started down the steps to my car.

"Wait," said Christina. "Let's sit down and smoke together before you go."

The part of me that was already on the freeway resisted. It was time to get on the road. It was time to get going.

"Come on," she urged, never hesitant to push a little to get her way.

We sat on the porch and looked out at the ocean reflecting the late afternoon sun, and smelled the pine tree that hung over the roof of the house, and caught a whiff of eucalpytus on the breeze mingled with the salt air, and smoked a pipe.

Those scattered parts of myself came back to the present and joined with the love of my friend, grounded in this moment, this place. My body relaxed. My mind calmed down. Now, I was ready to go.

The Mountain

Verde Valley, Arizona—Sometimes Linda and I would drive up to our favorite area on the mountain, park the truck, and then she'd go her way, hunting for fossils, and I would go mine. We'd meet up several hours later and share what we found. There weren't really trails in this area, so I'd just pick a path around the Prickly Pears and the Manzanita thickets, headed uphill.

After walking a little ways, I'd find a spot to sit—on a big rock, or a view spot looking over the valley with its green fields and band of Cottonwoods along the river, or I'd sit next to a plant I was drawn to: a stand of Manzanita, the brilliant magenta flowers of a Claret Cup cactus, the delicate, luminous flowers of White Evening Primrose, or in the shade of a Juniper. When ravens flew overhead I could hear the swoosh of their wings like a heavy breath in the air. Sometimes I gathered a few leaves or flowers, but usually I just sat there. After awhile, I'd reach into my pouch, take out my Otter pipe and fill it with some herbs, and share a smoke.

Mullein (*Verbascum Thapsus L.*)

The Plant People

"Navajo herbalist and WWII veteran Sam B. Boone prepares to gather essential ceremonial and medicinal herbs. He treats each plant in a gentle and respectful manner, solemnly addressing the spirit of the herb using the archaic name known only to special medicine men. He maintains absolute faith in the unfailing curative powers and kindness of the 'plant people.'"

Sam B. Boone, Navajo Herbalist
Introduction, Phyllis Hogan
Official Journal of the Arizona Ethnobotanical Research Association
Vol. 1, No. 2, p. 1
Summer Solstice, 1988

"I want to learn about herbs," is like saying,
"I want to learn about people."
The only way to do that
is to get to know individual people,
and individual herbs, one at a time.
Sometimes, it takes a long time
just to get to know one person, or one plant.

"Thus, contemplation on plants in general
or one particular plant species in particular
can be a path to understanding the sacred
in deeper ways and a way to learn
about what it means to be human."

Stephen Harrod Buhner
*Sacred and Herbal
Healing Beers,* p. 144

"The life of plants is considered very special,
or holy...It's like a human life...it's considered
as a living being that you can communicate through
and be understood, and have it understand you
as well. So, it's a very sacred involvement
when you gather plants..."

Jerome Jackson, Navajo Plant Gatherer
Official Journal of the Arizona Ethnobotanical Research Association
Vol. 2, No. 1, p. 5
Fall Equinox, 2000

"You ask their permission, and once you receive
their permission, you harvest just what you need,
and you give your thanks by giving something
back to the plants. Now that raises the question,
what do you give a plant?
And the answer is, what the plant wants.
So that's part of it. You have to find
out what is wanted, as a way of exchanging favors.
And that in itself begins to bring you
into relationship with the world."

Eliot Cowan
"Indigenous Medicine for Modern
Humans, An Interview
with Eliot Cowan"
by Erin Everett, *New Life Journal*
Oct/Nov 2001

"I was able to see the internal parts of the
chromosomes...It surprised me because
I actually felt as if I was right down there
and these were my friends...
As you look at these things [corn plants],
they become part of you.
And you forget yourself."

Barbara McClintock
1983 Nobel Laureate in Physiology or Medicine for her discovery of the ability of genes to change position on the chromosome in relation to their environment.

"There is only one active ingredient
in plant medicine—friendship."

Eliot Cowan
Plant Spirit Medicine, p. 20

"It may be futile to look for distinct chemical agents
in Native American medicine as explanation
for efficacy, because much of an herb's effect
may be due to ritual methods of gathering and usage.
At St. Regis, Mohawk Nation,
there are approximately 200 ways
of gathering plant medicine."

Ken Cohen (citing J.W. Herrick, D.R. Snow, eds. *Iroquois Medical Botany*, 1995, p. 35)
"Native American Medicine"
Alternative Therapies in
Health and Medicine, Nov. 1998, p. 9

A Gathering Story: Growling Coyote Mullein

"Nature is the human heart made tangible."
Marilou Awiakta

Verde Valley, Arizona—Linda had a routine of riding her bike around the corn field in the early morning, now that it was the height of summer. After finishing her ride one day, she burst into the house with "big news."

"You should see the Mullein on the other side of the corn field!" she exclaimed. "It's huge. We've got to go pick some of it. I would have done it, but it's pretty brushy and I didn't have my boots on."

Big brush meant the possibility of big snake. The other side of the corn field was closer to the Verde River and wilder, with a thick tangle of Cottonwood, Mesquite, Cat's Claw and tall brush. In the area where she had spotted the Mullein, she'd seen deer and elk last spring. Linda had grown up in the woods in Minnesota with a father and four brothers who were hunters and trappers and she had fine-tuned instincts for spotting animal wildlife.

A few days after Linda spotted the Mullein, we had an unexpected guest at the ranch: a man the owner had sent to do some construction and repairs. Prepared to be accommodating, we were shocked when he turned out to be intentionally rude and obnoxious and fiercely interested in establishing the ranch as his territory. He managed to goad both of us into uncharacteristic, angry reactions.

The first night he was there he got bit by an ant. The next day he poured poison on all the ant hills he could find around the property.

Ignoring his presence as best we could, Linda decided to go and collect some of the giant Mullein she'd seen. She was back sooner than I expected, out of breath and her eyes wide.

"I didn't get any Mullein. There was a big, beautiful coyote standing right next to it. But it was acting really strange. When it saw me, it didn't leave, it stood its ground and growled. That is very unusual behavior for a coyote. I've run across a lot of coyotes and never once has one growled at me."

I could see Linda was strongly affected by her encounter.

"I'm going to tell our neighbor," she said. He was a Fish and Game Officer. There had been several reports of rabies up in Flagstaff, but none in our area. Still, it was strange behavior for a coyote and she wanted to report it.

She told the owner, too, in case he was going to be over in that part of the field.

"What'd they say?" I asked.

She shook her head and shrugged.

"Oh they dismissed it, as usual. Because I'm a 'girl' they think I don't know what I'm talking about. Well, maybe it had pups.That might explain it."

The scene with the man got worse. He broke the water pipe he was supposed to be fixing and had to spend several days finding parts to repair it while the garden needed watering. His rudeness bordered on abusive and his constant blaring of a rock and roll radio station on the outside speakers ravaged the quiet harmony of our wilderness paradise.

We moved into a motel over the July 4th holiday while the owner came with a large group of friends and family, including the man, and stayed at the ranch. They had plans to build a screened porch.

When we returned, the radio music was still blaring and we heard a tale from the owner of a holiday filled with "near-disasters." Building the screened room had taken three times as long as planned because the measurements were wrong, they had to keep going into town, and things kept breaking. A guest drove the truck into a ditch and flooded the kayaks in the river, and a four-year-old child rode one of the ATVs into the irrigation canal and had to be rescued. Several people got stung by wasps and bit by spiders.

After they all left, Linda and I took a morning walk around the corn field—the first in several weeks since her encounter with the coyote. I was floating along in a blissful state, enjoying the cool morning, the sound of the birds, the damp, sweet smell of plants along the river—happy to be back, happy the man was gone.

"Where's the Mullein?" I asked.

"It's right up here..."

Her answer was shattered by ferocious, *enraged* snarling and growling coming from twenty feet away.

Inexplicably my body didn't tune into the fear wave-length.

"Oh I guess we'd better turn around," I said blithely, while every hair on Linda's body stood straight up.

We quickly walked back the way we'd come.

Delayed reaction set in. We both started to shake.

"That's the scariest encounter I've ever had with a wild animal," said Linda. "That coyote is either really sick or really hurt. It's a good thing you didn't tune into the fear thing. That probably saved our lives."

We told our neighbor and he got his gun and went hunting for the coyote, but he didn't find a trace. We talked about it sometimes, but we never did gather any Mullein from that plant.

Plant Neighbors

Tahlequah, Cherokee Nation—That summer the electric thunderstorms rolled through one after the other, sometimes lingering for a couple of weeks before they broke. I didn't mind the storms, the lightning crackling down all around our apartment, the rolls of thunder shaking the windows, and the rain falling through the sky in solid walls of water. It was the low barometric pressure that got me. That, and the mold. The local television weather station reported mold counts in the danger zone for two months straight.

Everyone was sick. Headaches, sore throats, achey joints, chest problems, coughs, sinus problems. You didn't want to walk outside. It felt dangerous. I could take the hundred degree heat and the hundred percent humidity, but I couldn't take the mold. Except for rapid forays across the street to the university library, without a car we were pretty much confined to the apartment. We drank gallons of iced coffee as an antidote. My sister turned white and pasty and lay on the couch, wasted.

Later, my sister told me the Cherokee belief that if there is an illness that arises in an environment, there will be an antidote growing nearby. Wondering if I could prove this, I remembered the plants I saw growing everywhere that summer—along the roadsides, in the cracks of sidewalks, in people's yards and driveways—and identified them as Mullein and Echinacea.

When I looked up in an herb book a remedy for mold, it said "Mullein and Echinacea." Now, I *always* check out what plants are living in my neighborhood.

Datura (*Datura* sp.)

Dangerous Smoke

Pay attention to the physical and energetic
properties of the plants you smoke.
Where did that plant come from?
How was it taken from the Earth?
Its energy will go straight to your brain.
That is the power of smoke. That is its gift.
You want that energy to be good.

There are two main ways
to hurt yourself with smoking.
One way is through the ignorant
or abusive use of Power Plants—
plants that have the transformative power
of Death/Rebirth, mentally, physically, or
spiritually. These would include *Nicotiana*, Datura,
Cannabis, and other powerful
psychotropic plants.

The other way is to smoke plants
which have been poisoned by added
toxic chemicals or negative energies. This would
encompass commercially grown tobacco
and marijuana, as well as some mass-produced
and processed herbs.

"A Navajo herbalist explained it to me this way,
'Tobacco is *Diyin*—Holy Person.
Use it with respect and it rewards you.
Use it the wrong way, it kills you.'"

Joseph Winter
Director, Native American
Plant Cooperative

"Datura (*cho hi jil yeh*) for example,
is a very dangerous plant
that can cause you to lose your mind...
Then it can cause death due to the process
of those negative affects to one's mind."

Jerome Jackson, Navajo Plant Gatherer
Official Journal of the Arizona Ethnobotanical Association
Vol. 2, No.1,
Fall Equinox, 2000

Growing, gathering, and processing
the traditionally sacred smoke plant
Nicotiana has been desecrated.

Note 1

"Huge amounts of pesticides are used on commercial tobacco: up to 16 applications may be made in three months. Pesticides used include those that are extremely and acutely toxic, cause cancer and birth defects and nerve damage...The United States Department of Agriculture tests tobacco only for pesticides no longer used in the United States such as DDT...No screening is done for residues of legal pesticides on tobacco."

Ellen Hickey and Yenyen Chan
Tobacco, Farmers and Pesticides: The Other Story

Global governmental policies have ensured
that almost all marijuana plants
are impregnated with the
energy properties of fear, power,
greed, and violence.

Lung cancer and other diseases linked to smoking in modern times did not appear in significant numbers until the cigarette rolling machine was invented. Native Americans of the Southwest who have traditionally smoked locally grown and gathered plants as part of their culture had a negligible incidence of tobacco-related illnesses until they began smoking commercial cigarettes.

Note 2

Tobacco (*Nicotiana* sp.)

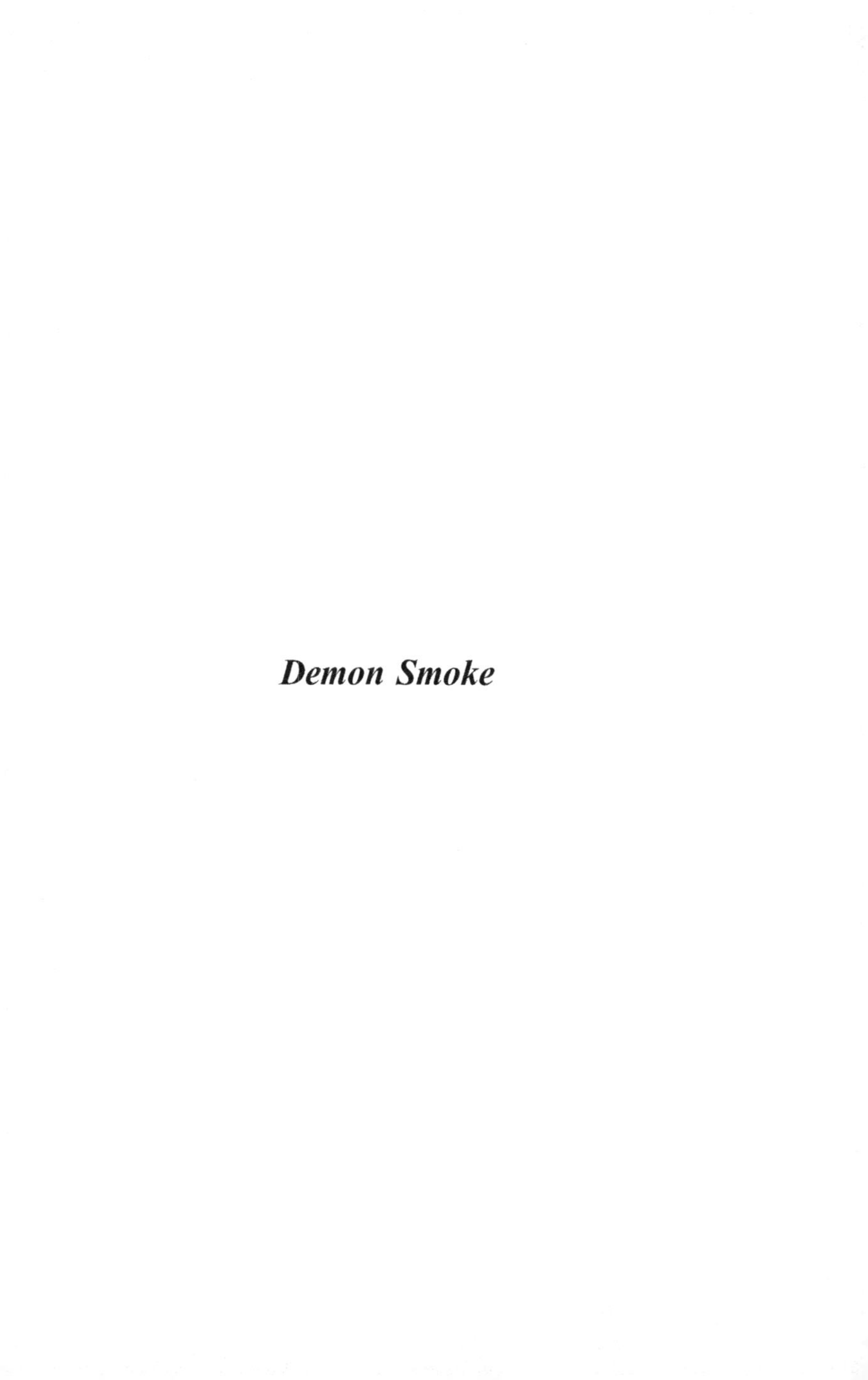

Demon Smoke

Smoking is _____ for you.

The act of smoking has been demonized.

Whatever a society desecrates, demonizes, and shames becomes its collective shadow.

What are the dangers of the shadow?
Acts of power which are forbidden
and banished to the shadows as “bad”
turn their power against us and control us
from the subconscious. These become
our cultural addictions and diseases.

Addictions are substitutes
for meaningful relationships. A healthy society
provides cultural pathways that
encourage respectful relationships
with every living thing.

"*Mi taka oyasin.*"
(All my relations.)

Said at the end of every
Lakota smoke ceremony.

The lack of healthy relationships
creates isolation, alienation and stress.
Stress is the primary disease of our culture.
Stress chemicals in our bodies
are causing an epidemic
of hormonal, immune, nervous system,
digestive, mental, and emotional illnesses.

Note 3

The medicinal remedies for stress
approved by our society
and our medical establishment are known
to be addictive and physically harmful.

Note 4

"It [pipe smoking] is one of the most venerable traditions of stress-reduction known to mankind..."

J.P. Beaumier & L. Camp
The Pipe Smoker, p. 52

The missing pieces of our wholeness
are always hidden in the shadow.

Red Osier Dogwood, Red Willow (*Cornus* sp.)

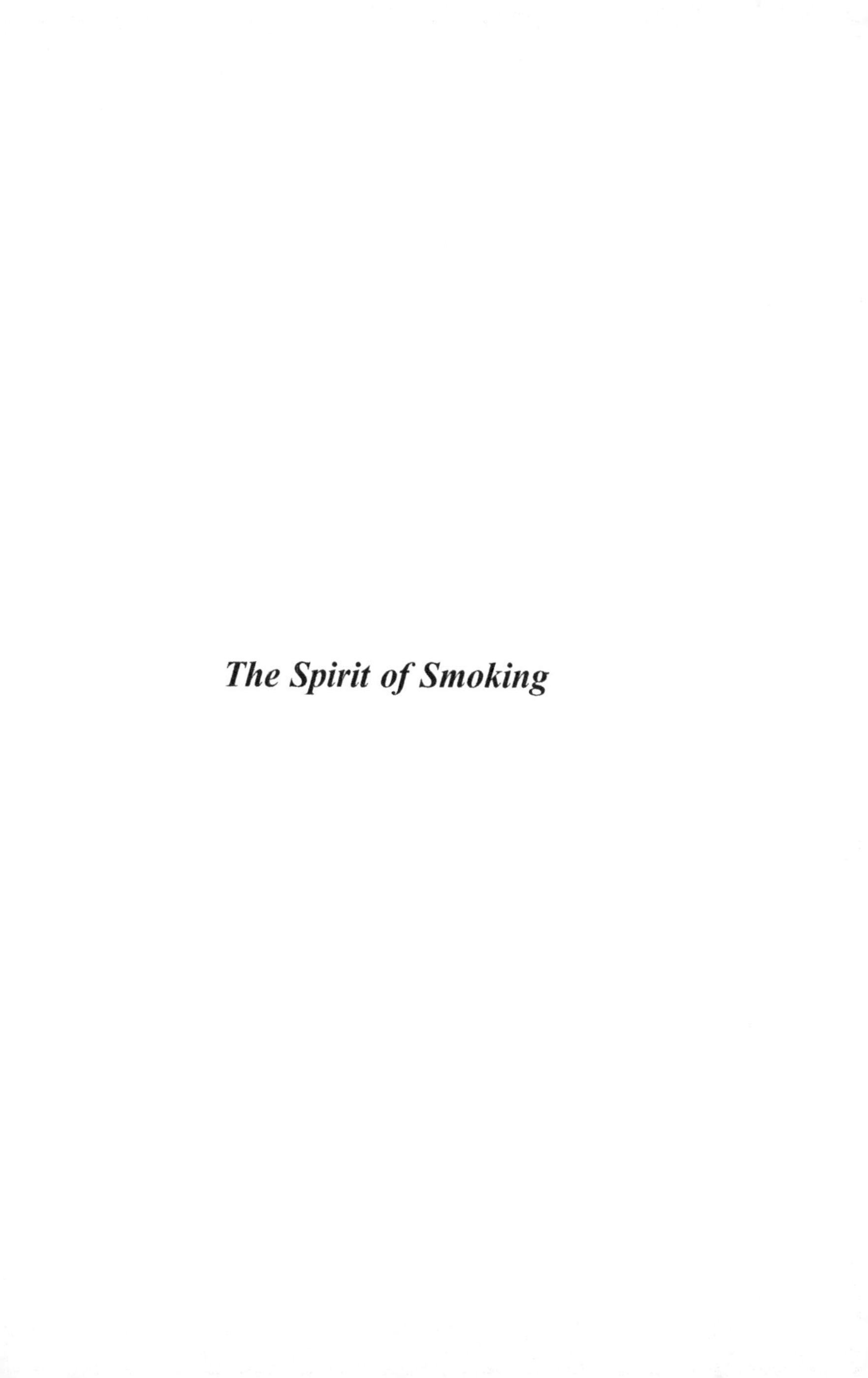

The Spirit of Smoking

The original spiritual purpose of smoking plants
was to communicate with Spirit.

"The mythic account of the giving of tobacco
in many Native traditions indicates that
communication with the spiritual powers,
the function of tobacco,
is the primary condition of life;
it comes before food itself."

Jordan Paper
Offering Smoke, p. 53

"All the world's major religious texts
contain innumerable instances
where holy teachers have used
the sacredness of plants as a teaching
to help human beings understand
the nature of the divine
and their relation to it."

Stephen Harrod Buhner
Sacred and Healing
Herbal Beers, p. 158

Lakota

"With visible breath I am walking,
A voice I am sending as I walk.
In a sacred manner I am walking.
With visible tracks I am walking.
In a sacred manner I walk."

White Buffalo Calf Woman
"The Offering of the Pipe"
Black Elk Speaks
John G. Neihardt, p. 4

Crow

"Sacred Spirit in the Sun,
it has been a long time
since you have smoked with me."

The Crow Indians
Robert H. Lowie, p.270

Blackfoot

"Sacred Person! Behold
I am still alive,
I ask the spirit of
the wild geese
to smoke with me,
The first that came
into this country,
I know of no medicine
as strong as my smoke."

The Old North Trail or Life, Legends and Religion of the Blackfeet
Walter McClintock, pp. 97-98

Pawnee

"It is now time to offer smoke to the gods
to show that we remember them..."

Skidi Pawnee Two Lance Society
Ritual warrior society renewal
of the lances
"Pawnee Indian Societies"
Anthropological papers of the American Museum of Natural History,
1914:561-567
James Murie

"But there was something he had to do
before he could rest.
He got up, filled and lighted the pipe,
and blew smoke to the east, then south,
then west, then north, then up, then down.
When he blew smoke
to each of the four corners, he prayed.
He prayed for health and long life.
He prayed to live to see his children
and his children's children.
Then he prayed that power be sent to him
and that it might be good power
and that he might use it right."

"Hunting for Power,
The Year of the Sun Dance on
No Arm's River (1863)"
The Ten Grandmothers
Alice Marriott, p. 45

It is not *about* smoking.
It is about having respectful relationships—
with plants, with Spirit, with ourselves,
and with each other.

"Now, my friend, let us smoke together
so that there may be only good between us."

Black Elk
Black Elk Speaks
John G. Neihardt, p. 6

Damiana (*Turnera diffusa*)

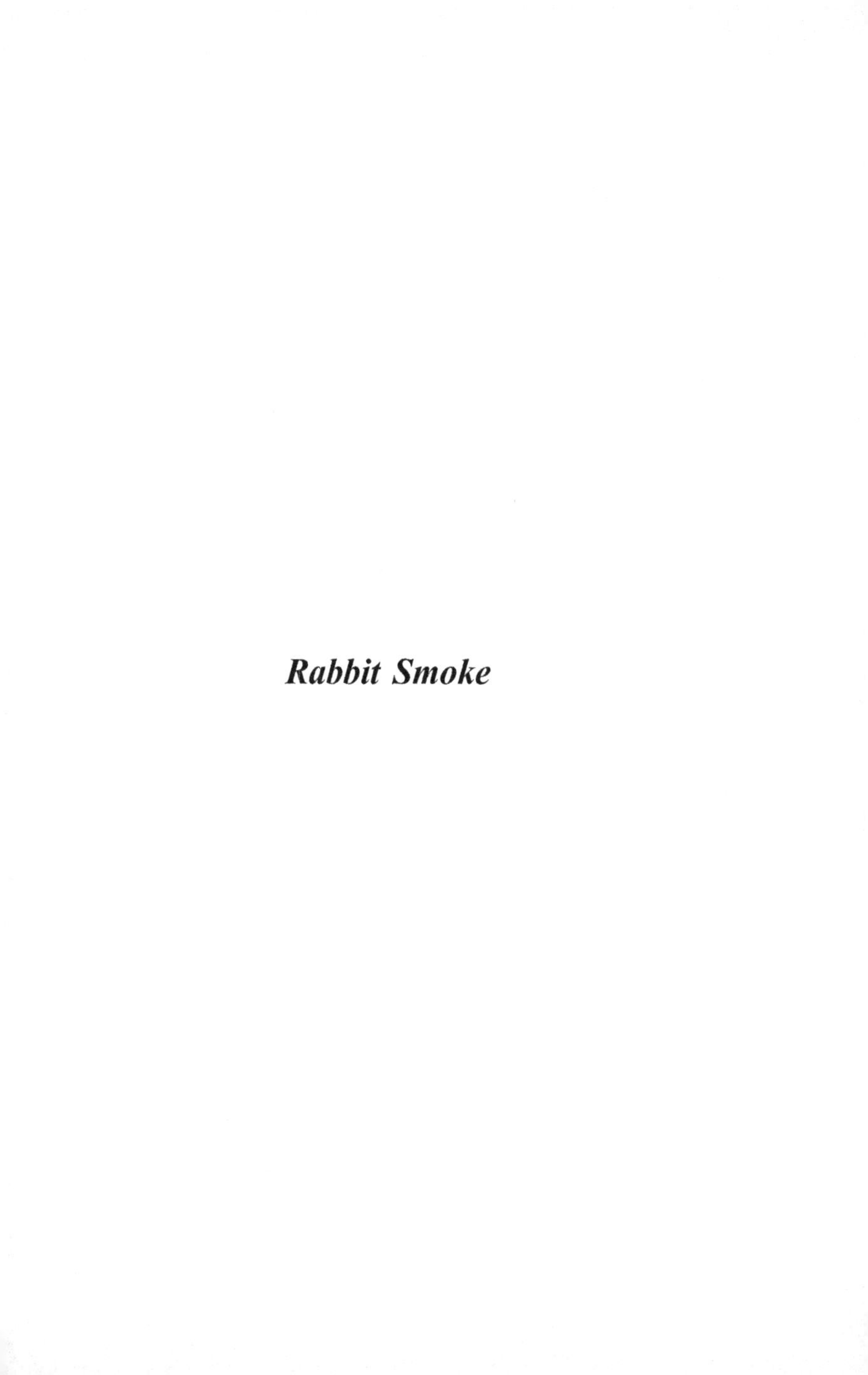

Rabbit Smoke

"A handsome Cheyenne woman walked up
to me at a fair in Arkansas as I stood
in the shade smoking my pipe.
'I smell Rabbit Smoke,' she said.
'Rabbit Smoke?' I asked.
'The Cheyenne say anything a rabbit nibbles
you can smoke. Yours smells good.'"

E.J.Young (Cherokee)

Not everything that is smoked is *Nicotiana*: "...a wide variety of other smoked substances...have been reported in the archaeological and ethnographic literature (Adams & Toll:151)", including over 60 different species known to have been smoked in eastern North America (von Gernet:74).

Karen Adams, Mollie Toll, Alexander von Gernet in *Tobacco Use by Native North Americans, Sacred Smoke and Silent Killer*

I am aware of no evidence that
occasional smoking of
non-addictive plant material in a pipe
is especially physically harmful.

The impact of smoking a wild plant
that you have respectfully gathered
and prepared yourself is profound.
A connection is established
between you and the "plant people."
You begin to trust that the plants of this Earth
are here to help you and heal you.
Remember to thank them.

Skullcap (*Scutellaria* sp.)

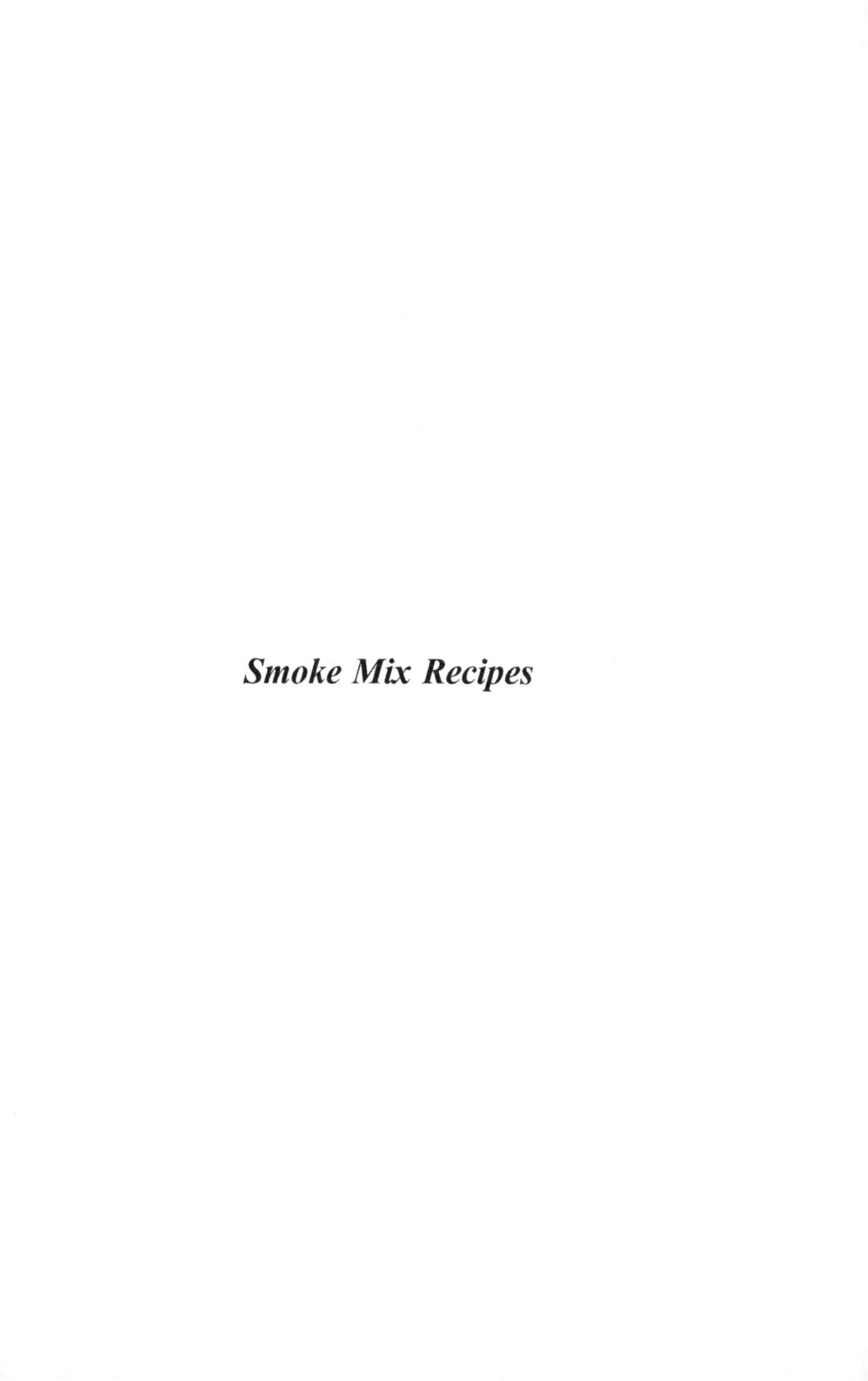

Smoke Mix Recipes

You don't have to know many plants to gather a good smoke mix from wild plants. Mullein is pretty easy to find, easy to prepare, and is a good base for almost any mix. Uva Ursi, Sumach or Manzanita can also be found without too much difficulty, depending on where you live. You can also purchase good herbs from organic growers or small, ethical wildcrafters, or grow them in window boxes and gardens. Michael Moore's Web site is a reliable source for good herbal companies and his books give you enough information to identify plants in the wild. Howie Brounstein, a contemporary herbalist, has excellent information on smoking herbs at his Web site. He suggests that keeping herbs slightly moist makes for a better smoke.

Spinning Coyote Smoke Mix

Mullein
Skullcap
Passionflower
Manzanita
Damiana
Fennel (or anise) seed

Good for insomnia, "spinning out," to stop or reduce marijuana smoking, and for anxiety and nervousness. A good end of the day or bedtime smoke or for relaxing with friends. A good smoke for those perfectionists who are addicted to the adrenaline and ego thrill of being really, really busy and have trouble slowing down.

Proportions: One half cup Mullein, one quarter cup each Skullcap and Passionflower, one eighth cup each Manzanita and Damiana, and a sprinkle of Fennel or Anise seeds to taste.

(You may use any other measuring container you want instead of a cup: a bowl, a basket, a plate, or a tray.)

E.J.'s Tahlequah Blend

Manzanita or Uva Ursi
Mullein
Sumach
Deer's Tongue
Sage
Mint

A hearty, flavorful smoke, good for cutting back on Tobacco or Marijuana smoking. The Deer's Tongue has a wonderful aroma, and Sumach gives it a good flavor. I'd never used Manzanita as a base, but when E.J. shared this one with me, I liked it a lot.

Proportions: One half cup Manzanita, one quarter cup each Mullein and Sumach, some Deer's Tongue, a bit of Sage and Mint.

Stoned Labyrinth

Hops
Mullein
Skullcap
Damiana
Fennel Seeds
Mint

I love the heavy, sensual calming effect of Hops and Skullcap together. Hops has a funny smell kind of like ripe cheese, but it smokes with a nice flavor and no aftertaste. The first time I smoked this mix with my women friends, we were talking about the stone labyrinth we had built, and as a matter of fact we were feeling a little stoned, so I named it after that. If you're feeling depressed, I'd smoke Spinning Coyote instead of Stoned Labyrinth. Hops has a tendency towards being a "downer" herb.

Proportions: One half cup Hops, one quarter cup Mullein, one eighth cup Skullcap, one eighth cup Damiana, a sprinkle of Fennel and Mint.

Take It Easy

Hops
Mullein
Manzanita
Skullcap
Deer's Tongue
Anise

Similar to Stoned Labyrinth but the Manzanita gives it a bit more edge and the Deer's Tongue gives it a great aroma. I blended this mix for a surfer friend of mine.

Proportions: One-half cup Hops, one-quarter cup Mullein, one-eighth cup Skullcap and Manzanita, Deer's Tongue to taste and a sprinkling of Anise.

Wild Gulch Mix

Mullein
Blackberry leaves
Mint

A mild, gentle smoke from plants growing in a moist wash near where I live. A nice summer smoke. And while you're at it, why not eat the Blackberries and make some iced Mint tea?

Proportions: Two-thirds cup Mullein, one-third cup Blackberry, a sprinkle of Mint.

Blackberry Mix

Mullein
Blackberry leaves
Blackberry root
Mint

The root gives this a bit more astringency.

Proportions: One-half cup Mullein, one-quarter cup Blackberry leaves, some Blackberry root to taste, and a sprinkle of Mint.

Beautiful Flowers Mix

Mullein
Passionflower
Dogwood
Sweet Clover

A relaxing smoke with a sweet aroma. All these are found near Tahlequah, in the Cherokee Nation. Dogwood trees bloom in the early spring before other flowers are out, and seeing their creamy white and pink blossoms surrounded by brown, bare branches gladdens the heart after a long winter.

Proportions: One-half cup Mullein leaves and flowers, one-quarter cup Passionflower, Dogwood bark to taste, a sprinkle of Sweet Clover.

Cough Mix

Mullein
A little Coltsfoot or Horehound

Mullein soothes the lungs and Coltsfoot or Horehound helps you cough and get the gunk out.

Proportions: Mainly Mullein with just a little of the expectorant herb.

Nixing Nicotine I

Mullein
Manzanita or Uva Ursi
Passionflower
Skullcap
A pinch of Lobelia

Lobelia connects to the same receptors as nicotine and helps you break the addiction. It is used (as lobeline) in the chewing gum that helps people stop smoking. You can get Lobelia from any good herb store. Use for a couple of weeks and then just use the straight mix without Lobelia. Mullein helps clean out the lungs, which is why I like to put it in all my mixes. Skullcap and Passionflower will help settle the nerves.

Proportions: One-half cup Mullein, one-quarter cup each Manzanita (or Uva Ursi), Passionflower, and Skullcap. Use just a pinch of Lobelia. It's all you need. More is not better!

Nixing Nicotine II

Mullein
Hops
Willow Bark
Mint
A pinch of Lobelia

The Hops gives a nice, heavy calming effect and the Willow adds a heartiness for people accustomed toTobacco. Mullein helps clean the lungs.

Proportions: One-half cup Mullein, one-third cup Hops, one-quarter Willow bark, add Mint to taste and a pinch of Lobelia.

Nellie Bly Nettle Mix

Nettles
Mullein
Skullcap
Fennel seeds
Mint

Nettles grow along a road in our gulch called Nellie Bly Lane, the site of an old mining claim named after the famous nineteenth-century entrepreneur, writer, and adventurer. All of these smoke plants grow in the gulch except Skullcap, which I'm determined to find. Jamie and I collect the Nettles and boil them for a green vegetable, make beer and vinegars from them, and I use them for smoke mixes. Nettles are very high in calcium and have properties that help arthritis. I'm not sure if any of these properties transfer in the smoke.Wear gloves to collect. When they are dry they don't sting. I still wear the gloves to crush them though.

Proportions: One-half cup Nettles, one-quarter cup Mullein and Skullcap, Fennel seeds and Mint to taste.

Sweet and Sexy

Mullein
Hops
Damiana
Fennel or Anise seeds

Damiana helps open the sexual channels and Hops brings you into that nice, slow, sensual place.

Proportions: One-half cup Mullein, one-third cup Hops, one-quarter cup Damiana, sprinkle Fennel or Anise seeds to taste.

Traditional Kinnik kinnik
(without Nicotiana)

Red Willow
Uva Ursi
Spicebush

I am less familiar with the barks, but they were a primary ingredient in most traditional mixes.

Proportions: Equal parts Red Willow bark and Uva Ursi, Spicebush to taste.

Philosopher's Mix

Mullein
Sumach
Uva Ursi
Sage
Deer's Tongue
Cedar

A delicious smelling mix, rich and deep. Good for contemplation on deep thoughts.

Proportions: One-half cup Mullein, one-quarter cups Sumach and Uva Ursi, Sage, Cedar and Deer's Tongue to taste.

Mullein Sprout (*Verbascum Thapsus L.*)

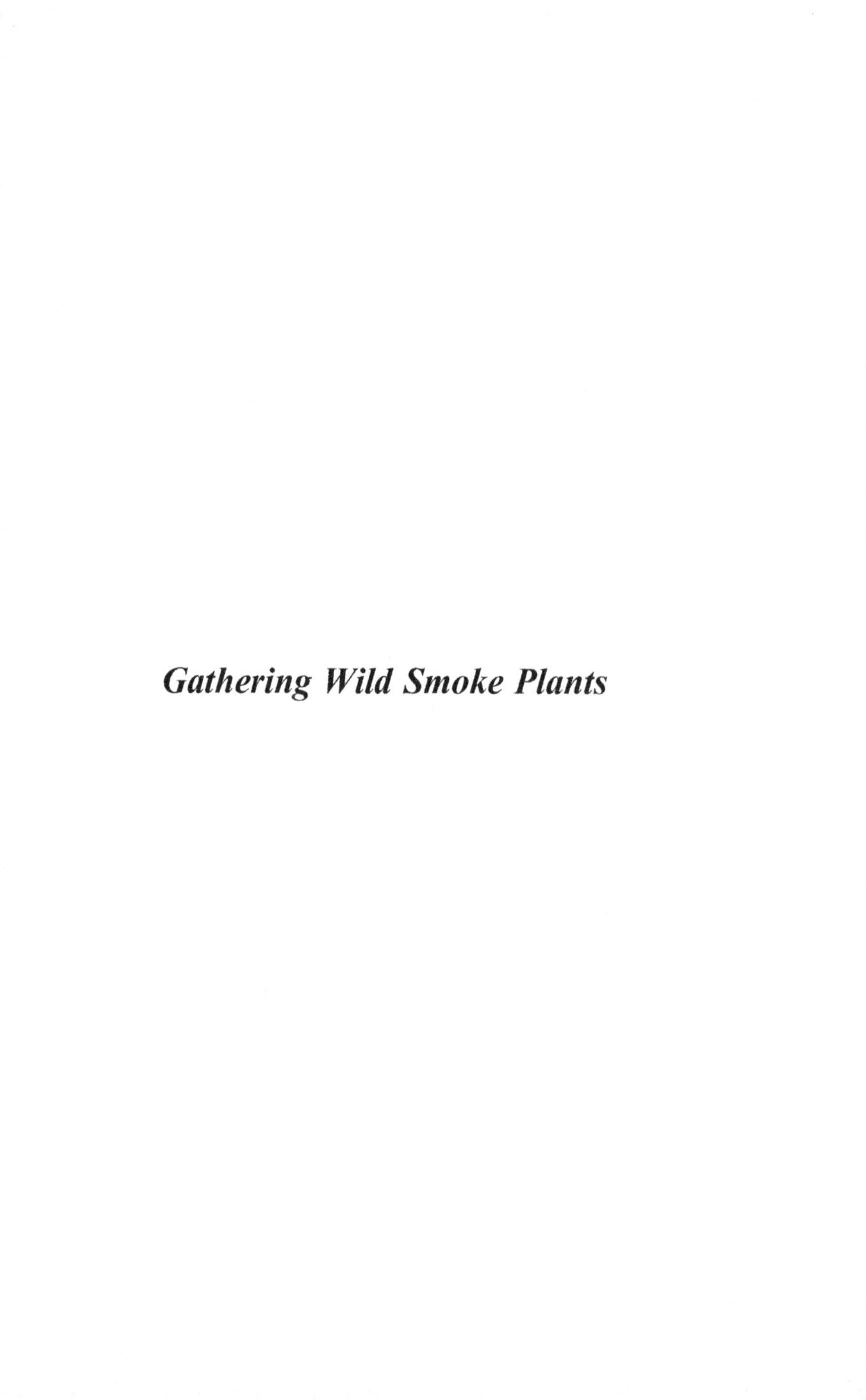

Gathering Wild Smoke Plants

Gathering Ethics: Be knowledgeable, be respectful, don't be greedy.

SMOKING LEAVES

Bearberry, Uva-Ursi

Arctostaphylos uva-ursi
Kinnik kinnik (Ojibwe), *Saga Komin agun* (Chippewa)
Description: Small, leathery, oval or heart-shaped leaves with pronounced center veins. The plant is a mat or vine which grows to about eight or ten inches high. Reddish brown, shredded bark on stems. Habitat is high mountains, in open clearings. Some strains found along sandy slopes of Pacific beaches from California to Alaska.
Preparation: Dried leaves are usually smoked, sometimes bark and roots. Break into small pieces when dry.
Properties: A fine, thick smoke, astringent, mild enough to smoke alone (Brounstein). Used for nervous system by the Chippewa in traditional usage (Densmore). One of the most commonly smoked plants throughout North America by First Nations for prayer and recreational use (Indian Country).

Bent Grass

Agrostis palustris Huds
Johonaa'el Binat'oh, Sun Smoke (Navajo)
Description: Perennial grass with stems 6-20 inches

tall. Leaves are one to three inches long and rough to touch. Found in moist areas such as stream beds and springs at 3,600 to 7,200 feet.

Preparation: Dry and crush leaves and smoke.

Properties: "This herb is also mixed with other plants to make Beauty Way smoke, *Hoozhonee Nat'oh* (Boone)."

Blackberry

Rubus sp.

Description: Dark green, five leaves, reddish thorned stems, bushes two to three feet high, underside of leaves is stickery, grows in "briar patches" where there is moisture.

Preparation: Dry leaves, crush, and add to smoking mixtures.

Properties: The leaves are very gentle and can be added to smoke mixtures (Brounstein).

Coltsfoot

Tussilago farfara

Description: The broad, sea-green leaves resemble the White Poplar. Flowering stem with whitish hairs and a yellow flower appears before the leaves. Seeds are crowned with a tuft of silky hairs.

Preparation: Dry leaves and mix with other herbs.

Properties: Used as an expectorant to promote coughing, good for lung cleansing. Do not use when you cannot stop coughing, use Mullein instead (Brounstein). Added to smoking mixtures with Red

Willow Bark, Uva Ursi, Damiana and Manzanita (Winter Sun). Smoking of the leaves for a cough has been recommended by the ancient herbalists Dioscorides, Galen, Pliny, and Linnaeus. Smoked to relieve asthma in British Herb Tobacco which also included Buckbean, Eyebright, Betony, Rosemary, Thyme, Lavender, and Chamomile flowers (Grieve).

Damiana

Turnera diffusa

Description: A shrub which can reach six feet in height. The stems are slender, smooth, straight and yellow or reddish-brown. Small, inch-long leaves grow in clusters alternately along the stem. The underside of the leaves are lightly covered with whitish hairs. Little yellow flowers. Habitat is around the Gulf of Mexico, especially in Baja California near Todos Santos.

Preparation: Mix dried leaves with other herbs for smoking. Harvest leaves and tops while the plant is in flower and dry in the shade. Pick out twigs.

Properties: Gentle nervine and relaxant. Traditionally used as a gentle sexual stimulant. Used in smoking mixtures (Winter Sun). It has a lovely, sweet aroma, but too much can be harsh. This is one of my favorites.

Deer's Tongue, Wild Vanilla

Liatris odoratissima

Description: Perennial herb. Has fleshy, oblong basal

leaves ending in a flattened stalk. The flowers are a vivid purple. Its lovely aroma is due to crystals of Coumarin which can be seen on the upper side of the smooth, spatulate leaves. Habitat is from Virginia south. Flowers in September and October.
Preparation: Dry leaves. Break up into small pieces.
Properties: Sweet aroma. Leaves are used to flavour Tobacco (Grieve).

Dittany, Mountain Dittany, Stonemint

Cunila origanoides
Description: Perennial plants with small flowers in clusters. Calyx is very hairy. Leaves are oval, serrate, nearly an inch long. Prefers dry and rocky hill-sides from New York to Georgia and westward.
Preparation: Dry leaves. Use for flavor and aroma.
Properties: Very aromatic, warming, pungent and relaxing.

Golden Eye (Sunflower Compositae)

Viguiera sp.
Dine'ee Nat'oh, Deer Way Tobacco (Navajo)
Description: Herbs or shrubs with leafy, branched stems, opposing leaves and numerous yellow flowers.
Preparation: Unclear from Boone's description if you smoke leaves and/or flowers.
Properties: Used to ward off any feelings of bad thoughts, to guard against bad spirits, and to bless the sheep. This herb is a tobacco used in the *Dine'ii*, Deer Way Ceremony (Boone).

Life Everlasting, American Everlasting, Cudweed

Antennaria margaritaceum

Description: Linear, lance-shaped leaves with alternate stalk branched at the top, root perennial. Stalks are downy with white flowering branches forming a flat broad bunch, each branch with numerous heads.

Preparation: Dry leaves, use for smoking

Properties: Not known.

Lobelia, Red Lobelia, Indian Tobacco,

Lobelia inflata, L. cardinalis

Description: Red Lobelia is found in the wild near running water and springs, from 3,500 feet to 7,000 feet or higher. Found in the mountain West but not the lower parts of New Mexico, western Arizona, and eastern California. It is a slender plant with lance-shaped leaves and inch-long, bright red flowers along the end of the stem. The flowers are bright and easily seen. *Lobelia inflata* have hairy, ovate leaves and tiny light blue or whitish flowers, one quarter inch long. Native from Labrador south to Georgia and Arkansas.

Preparation: Dry leaves and flowers, crush or break up into small pieces. *Lobelia cardinalis* is not nearly as potent as *Lobelia inflata*. If you are using *Lobelia inflata,* use only a pinch mixed with other herbs such as Mullein. Use only a couple of pinches of *Lobelia cardinalis* mixed with other herbs.

Properties: Antispasmodic effects on the bronchials

and can be helpful as a smoke for asthmatics when smoked at the first sign of spasms (Moore/Mountain). Useful for breaking a nicotine habit as it connects to the nicotine receptors and helps during the nicotine withdrawal phase (Brounstein). Cherokee smoked to break the Tobacco habit (Hamel and Chiltoskey).

Manzanita

Arctostaphylos sp.

Description: Shrubs with beautiful, smooth, red bark, twisted branches, oval, dull green, leathery leaves. Varies in height from three to thirty feet. Forms thickets. Habitat is California and coastal mountains and as far east as parts of New Mexico and Texas.

Preparation: Collect any time, hang branches upside down, strip leaves off stem when dry, break leaves into small pieces to smoke.

Properties: Strong body and flavor, astringent, mix in small amounts with other herbs. Looks and tastes similar to Uva Ursi, but stronger flavor. Blended with other plants for prayer and recreational use by Western and Northwestern First Nations (Brounstein). Used by the Navajo (Winter). Cahuilla mixed leaves with Tobacco (Bean and Saubel). This was one of the plants used as a base for smoke mixes by almost all the First Nations. Interestingly, none of the references make any note of its properties other than "astringent."

Mullein

Verbascum Thapsus L.

Deer Ears (Navajo)
Description: Rounded, light green, fuzzy leaves in a basal rosette. Second year, a tall stem grows one to six feet tall. Found on waste ground, along roadsides. Common but sporadically located in central and northern Arizona, widespread in Rockies and West.
Preparation: Hang branches upside down to dry, strip leaves from stem, then chop, cut or rub leaves. The fuzziness can be itchy, so you might want to use cotton gloves and wear a long-sleeved shirt over your clothes. Flowers can also be smoked.
Properties: Soothes inflamed lungs, acts as expectorant. A very light, mild smoke, gentle, non-toxic. Used as a base in smoke mixes (Brounstein). Has been smoked for centuries (Moore/Mountain). It is a *Dine'ee nat'oh*, Deer Way Tobacco, and used in the Deer Way ceremony of the Navajo (Boone, Jackson). Helps blend other herbs. One of the friendliest smoke plants. I include it in all my mixes. Along with the Dogwoods, Manzanita and Sumach, it is traditionally one of the most frequently smoked plants. In addition to its beneficial effects on the lungs, the Navajo and Hopi used it to help heal the mind (Vestal, Whiting).

Nettle, Stinging Nettle

Urtica dioca
Description: Large, dark green leaves with serrated edges and stinging hairs on leaves and square-stemmed stalks. Can grow over six feet in height. Grows in patches, especially near streams and water. Found

across North America.
Preparation: Gather leaves with thick leather gloves! Hang to dry. The stinging hairs are rendered harmless when dry or cooked. Crumble leaves to smoke.
Properties: Used as a smoke plant in Europe and North America (Weed).

Pink Pussytoes, Pussytoes

Antennaria rosea Greene, A. neglecta, A. aprica
Coyote Bed (Navajo)
Description: Range is across the Midwest and Northeastern United States as far west as Colorado and south to Oklahoma and Arkansas.
Preparation: Leaves used in the tobacco mixture by the Blackfoot (Johnston) and Navajo (Winter).
Properties: Used as ceremonial medicine and in smoke mixes.

Pipsissewa and Pyrola

Chimaphila sp. *and Pyrola* sp.
Description: In the West, small evergreen plants, four to ten inches tall, with shiny, leathery leaves in loose whorls along tough stems. Can be found in moist, shady glens and well forested slopes, growing in leaf and needle mulch. In the East, often known as Wintergreen.
Preparation: Dry and break up into little pieces.
Properties: Similar in pharmacology to Uva Ursi and Manzanita but much less astringent. They add body to the smoking mix, yet are very mild. You can also smoke them alone (Brounstein). Favorite smoking to-

bacco of the Blackfoot (Johnston).

Raspberry

Rubus sp.

Description: Seldom more than three or four feet tall, prickly. In Arizona and the Rockies grows mostly on moist slopes and above streams at higher elevations above Ponderosa belt. In California, found along streams and in moist areas from almost sea level to 6,000 feet.

Preparation: Collect the large-leafed stems or branches just before and during flowering. Hang upside down to dry. Strip leaves with gloves on after drying. Cut into fine pieces with scissors or rub leaves between gloved hands like Sage or Mullein.

Properties: Light, mildly astringent smoke.

Sage, White Sage, Black Sage, Purple Sage, Garden Sage

Salvia dorii, S. carnosa Dougl

Navajo Prayer Smoke, Beautiful Smoke, Gray Tobacco (Navajo)

Description: Member of the mint family, has square stems and opposing leaves with long oblong rounded shape. Many varieties. Aromatic. Habitat from the Pacific to western borders of the Mohave, lower mountains of southern California, Arizona and New Mexico. Occasionally found in Rockies, Utah, and Idaho.

Preparation: Dry leaves and crush.

Properties: Used as sacred tobacco in both Navajo

and Hopi prayer smoke (Boone, Jackson, Winter Sun). Adds flavor and aroma to smoke mixes (Brounstein).

Sagebrush, Mugwort, Wormwood

Artemisia sp.

Description: Shrubs and small plants. Perennials can be collected anytime. Leaves tend to be hairy, lance shaped or deeply cleft or irreglarly fingered. Size varies.

Preparation: Rub or crush dried leaves.

Properties: Deep in historical references, said to promote dreams. Most *Artemisias* are strongly aromatic. Can be smoked alone but has strong flavor, so best to use lightly (Brounstein). Sagebrush is *not* Sage, which is milder. Sagebrush is burned and the smoke used ceremonially to purify the environment and used in sweats. Has anti-bacterial properties for airborne bacteria. A number of cultures smoke *Artemisia* (Buhner). Used as part of the smoke mix by Cahuilla, Pomo, Lakota and others (Moerman).

Skullcap

Scutellaria sp.

Description: Member of mint family with square stems. Found in moist rock crevices, meadow edges from 2,000 to10,000 feet. About eighteen inches in height, they are perennials and will grow back after cutting.

Preparation: Use leaves before completely dry, while still green if possible.

Properties: Skullcap is a calming herb to smoke. Good for insomnia, nervousness, anxiety, spinning out, and as a muscle relaxant (Brounstein). One of my personal favorites. I find it very grounding. Purchase Skullcap from small, reliable herb sellers as many of the large commercial sellers substitute European Germander, which is toxic to the liver when ingested.

Spicebush

Lindera benzoin

Description: One of the earliest fragrant, flowered shrubs to bloom in the spring. It has yellow flowers in tight clusters that appear long before the leaves. The flowers have six yellow sepals and a spicy aroma. Found in moist areas, along streams, low forests. Found in the Southeast and north to Missouri.

Preparation: Dry leaves, crush and add to smoke mix (Cowasuck).

Properties: The crushed leaves have a strong, lemony aroma.

Strawberry

Frugaria sp.

Description: Three-lobed, dark green leaves, pretty little white and yellow flowers, little strawberries, grows eight to nine inches high.

Preparation: Dry leaves, crush and add to smoking mixtures.

Properties: Mild, slightly astringent smoke.

Sumach, Smooth Sumach, Staghorn

Sumach

Rhus glabra, R. typhina

Description: Smooth Sumach forms stands of waist- and head-high plants with compound leaves of up to 31 to 33 leaves that turn bright red in the fall. Smooth Sumach grows in moist canyonlands of Arizona and New Mexico from 4,500 to 7,000 feet, north in warm canyons of Colorado, Utah to Canada, and east to the Atlantic Ocean.

Preparation: Some sources say traditionally gathered when leaves turn red in the fall (Paper). Harvested in autumn after the sun has burned it dry and the frost has nipped it (Louis Philippe). Smoke the dried, crushed leaves. Early references to also smoking the berries (Louis Philippe). Berries were also smoked (Cowasuck).

Properties: Smoked by many Nations and is one of the most frequently mentioned smoke plants in eighteenth-century descriptions of encounters with original inhabitants of North America by Europeans. Woodland Nations smoked for flavor (Indian Country) .

Sweet grass

Hierochloe odorata

Description: A winter-hardy aromatic perennial grass that grows in rich, moist soil from Alaska to Newfoundland and the northern states of the United States. It is a sacred plant in both North America and Europe. There is probably no truly "wild" sweetgrass left, having been cultivated for the last 10,000 years. Does not

normally produce viable seeds. It has been selected to have two harvests a year of its long leaves. Grows in moist meadows, marshes and along streams and lakes in North America, usually with other grasses.
Preparation: Dry leaves, crush, and add to other smoke herbs. The scent develops after leaves have dried, the fresh leaves are nearly scentless during the spring when plants are growing.
Properties: Burned for incense to purify the air and as ceremonial smudge. Also added to pipe smoking mixture (Winter Sun). Given for the Pipe in creation myth of the Cree (Paper).

Sweet Gum

Liquidambar styraciflua
Description: The Sweet Gum tree is found south of Connecticut to Florida and west to southern Illinois, Oklahoma, and eastern Texas. It has large leaves with five or seven-pointed lobes and fine-toothed edges. In spring, clusters of very small flowers appear and in the fall, brown balls of fruit and winged seeds. May grow up to 120 feet high.
Preparation: An early reference notes that the Indians smoked Tobacco mixed with leaves of the Sweetgum, dried and rubbed to pieces. Others mention that the gum was used for smoking at the court of the Mexican emperors.
Properties: Not known.

Yarrow

Achillea sp.

Description: Found throughout the United States. The leaves are delicate and fern-like, the flowers are white and umbrella-like but with a flat top.
Preparation: Dry and smoke leaves (Cowasuck).
Properties: Used as a medicinal, healing and magical herb throughout the world. Cherokee smoked for catarrh (Hamel and Chiltoskey).

Yerba Santa

Eriodictyon sp.
Description: All species have greasy, pleasant smelling leaves, alternate thick, slightly notched leaves and stems with a sticky varnished surface. Bushes, between two and six feet in height. Habitat is California coastal ranges, north to Oregon and Nevada, south to Baja California, drier slopes of the Sierra Nevadas, Arizona in lower mountains. from 1,000 to 6,000 feet (Moore/Mountain).
Preparation: Hang branches with leaves upside down to dry. Crush leaves for smoking.
Properties: For mild bronchial spasms, smoking the leaves along with the tea can improve the effects (Moore/Mountain). Used with Damiana and Coltsfoot to quit Tobacco habit (Winter Sun).

SMOKING FLOWERS

Betony, Lousewort, Elephant's Head, Parrot's Beak, Indian Warrior

Pedicularis sp.

Description: Resembles Snapdragon flowers. Usually found at highest elevations of major ranges in a moist, rain forest environment.
Preparation: Collect the whole flowering stalks, hang upside down to dry, use flowers that dry into buds that look a lot like marijuana buds.
Properties: Tranquilizers and muscle relaxants of varying strengths depending on variety. Very flavorful addition to smoke mixes (Brounstein).

Goldenrod

Solidago graminifolla, S. canadensis
Blue Lizard Tobacco (Navajo)
Description: Large, six-feet tall plants with flowering plumes of golden flowers. Native to eastern and southeastern United States.
Preparation: Pick flowers, dry and smoke.
Properties: Listed in early references as a native smoke plant (Hudson). Also used by the Navajo (Winter). Specific properties not known.

Hops

Humulus americanus
Description: A vine sometimes climbing on Poplars or Willows or forming dense trailing mats down moist slops. "Hops" are not really flowers but plump, oval cylinders called strobiles formed by overlapping light scales, about an inch long, light yellowish green to amber color. These Hops form open clusters on the ends and undersides of the stems. The native species found in Utah, Arizona, and the Rockies from New

Mexico northwards, from 5,500 feet to over 9,000 feet in very moist forest, edges of forest meadows, and along streams (Moore/Mountain).
Preparation: Pick Hops in early fall. Dry as soon after picking as possible since they darken and mildew easily. Better to dry with very low heat, 125-150 degrees in the oven with door slightly ajar on a burlap bag (Moore/Mountain).
Properties: Sedative, calming effect (Brounstein). I find it calming in a solid way. It has somewhat of a strange, cheesey smell, but a very good, soft flavor when you smoke it. You can actually get a little stoned from smoking good Hops. Good for insomnia. Not the best choice if you are depressed, however.

New England Aster

Aster Novae Anglia L.
Description: Native to eastern United States. Habitat is damp thickets and meadows. Grows to three to seven feet, flowers about one inch across, forty rays, intense purple color around a yellow disk. Found in almost all states except those in the far West, Texas, Louisiana, and Florida.
Preparation: Dry and smoke flowers (Cowasuck).
Properties: Not known.

Passionflower

Passiflora incarnata, P. foetida, P tenuiloba, P. mexicana
Description: Vines with palmate leaves. Identifiable by beautiful, exotic flowers that may be pink, purple,

or blue. The flowers have five sepals and five petals with a distinctive fringe of hairs that emerges from the calyx. Very striking. Native and cultivated Passionflowers may be found along mountain streams, roadsides, fences, inner city alleys, gardens.

Preparation: Dry leaves and flowers, crush and smoke.

Properties: A gentle sedative, very calming, good for nervousness (Brounstein). Some say you get "high" on it, but I only notice a nice relaxation of the nerves.

Pearly Everlasting, Ladies Tobacco

Anaphalis margaritacea

Description: Leaves are gray-green to wooly white, narrow, three to four inches long, no fragrance, alternately arranged on stem, often covered with fine spider web-like silk. Individual, erect stems grow one to three feet tall and are often in clumps. Globular flowers are long lasting, white, arranged around a yellow center. Found along dry trails, prairies, and throughout open areas and woods. (Life Everlasting, *Gnaphalium polycephalum*, is similar but with very fragrant leaves and earlier bloom. Used for asthma by the Rappahannock). Found just about everywhere in the United States.

Preparation: Crushed blossoms mixed with Mint (for men) or Marigold or Prairie Sage for women and used as a smudge or smoked (Johnstone).

Properties: Cherokee smoke plant (Hamel and Chiltoskey). Ojibwa used as a smudge for stroke (Smith).

Scotch Broom, Spanish Broom

Cytisus scoparius, Spartium junceum

Description: Scotch Broom grows to ten feet with many erect, slender, almost leafless branches. The flowers are small (about three quarters of an inch) and yellow and bloom from March to June. It is naturalized in California. Spanish Broom is similar with yellow flowers followed by four-inch pods. Blooms from June to September in most of the United States. In California it flowers most of the year. These Brooms often naturalize on dry, rocky slopes in the West.

Preparation: Gather flowers and put in a sealed, glass jar for ten days and then dry at low heat. The aging reduces harshness of the smoke. The flowering tops may be gathered in May without aging (Grubber).

Properties: I haven't tried them, but some sources say they have psychotropic properties due to their alkaloid content (Grubber).

Sweet Clover

Melilotus officinalis, M. alba

Description: Three-leafed clover growing from two to five feet in height, sometimes larger along stream beds. Miles of mountain roadsides often covered with the plants. Yellow and white blossoms.

Preparation: Dry leaves and flowers and add to smoke mixes (Cowasuck).

Properties: "The leaves...make a pleasant adjunct to pipe tobacco or as an aromatic addition to herbal smoking mixtures (Moore/Mountain)."

Yarrow

Achillea sp.

Description: (See Yarrow under Smoking Leaves.)

Preparation: Dry flower heads.

Properties: Used in mixture smoked in Ojibwa medicine lodge ceremonies (Smith).

SMOKING BARKS

Traditional preparation of bark for smoking:
Cut stems of Red Osier Dogwood, Flowering Dogwood, or Willow. Scrape off outer bark with knife. With back of knife blade, scrape curlicues of inner bark from the stem. Dry curlicues. Traditionally, a small rack was erected above a low fire so bark is about a foot above the flames and can dry without being burned. After about twenty minutes over fire, bark will be toasted and crisp and can be pulverized to consistency of rough-cut tobacco by rubbing it between palms. (Indian Country). Perhaps toasting in a slow oven would have similar results?

Dogwood, Red Osier (Creekside) Dogwood, Flowering Dogwood, Red Willow

Cornus sp.

Can'sa'sa (Cowasuck)

Description: A beautiful flowering small tree with creamy white and pink flowers. Found in Woodlands areas.

Preparation: Inner bark, roasted and shredded. Commonly mixed with Bearberry and Lovage Root (Cowasuck). Dried leaves are also smoked.
Properties: One of the most frequently used smoke mix ingredients by Native Americans. Documented use by Blackfoot, Ojibwa, Menominee, Cowasuck, Dakota, Lakota, Omaha, Pawnee, Winnebago, Ponca, Micmac, Cheyenne, Hoh, Salish, Cree, Meskwaki, Chippewa, Gosiute, and others. Among the Gosiute Indians, it ranked in importance with the tobacco plant proper (Chamberlin). The only smoking material referred to by Black Elk (Winter). Adds body to the smoke mix. Too raspy to smoke alone (Brounstein).

Gray Birch

Betula populifolia
Description: Trees in northeastern Unitd States. Wet to dry woods. A narrow, columnar, single-or multi-trunked tree, 35-50 feet tall. The white, non-peeling bark gets darker with age.
Preparation: Bark (Cowasuck).
Properties: Not known.

Willow

Salix sp.
Description: There are many varieties of Willow with a variety of bark colors: yellow, gray, blackish, brown. Leaves are thin, lance-shaped and the trees bear catkins in the spring. Found near water.
Preparation: See above. Collect by stripping bark

from the newer, smooth-barked branches. Dry and cut into thin strips.
Properties: Salicylate effects that act like aspirin to reduce inflammation do not transfer through smoking. Each Willow has different flavor and texture and give body and heartiness to smoking mixtures (Brounstein). One of the most commonly used plants for smoking among the First Nations (Indian Country). Used by the Chippewa in smoke mixes (Densmore). I find the Willows a little too astringent for me, but if you're used to a strong smoke, you'll probably like them.

SMOKING ROOTS

American Angelica, Great Purple Angelica

Angelica atropurpurea
Description: Native to eastern North America. Grows six to twelve feet tall, biennial. Has giant leaves, purple stems, and enormous white flowering umbels.
Preparation: Dig the root in the autumn, dry rapidly and place in air-tight container. If roots are thick, slice longitudinally to hasten drying. Pulverize and add to other smoking herbs.
Properties: When dry, the root is grayish brown and wrinkled. The odor is strong with a warm aromatic taste. Mendocino smoked root for colds (Chestnut) and Pomo medicine person smoked root shavings when doctoring (Goodrich and Lawson).

Aster

Aster puniceus

Description: Daisy-like flowers, generally recognisable by the combination of hairy stem and clasping leaves. Petals are light violet or violet blue. Grows two to seven feet. Sometimes called Christmas Daisies because they bloom so late in the year—August to November. Grows in moist meadows and roadside ditches from Manitoba, Canada southward to Georgia, Alabama, and Iowa.

Preparation: Pulverize fine tendrils of root, mix with other herbs, and smoke (Densmore).

Properties: Chippewa smoked to attract game (Densmore).

Blackberry

Rubus sp.

Description: (See Blackberry in Smoking Leaves.)

Preparation: Powder the root and mix well.

Properties: Blackberry root is a strong astringent that has use in smoking mixtures (Brounstein).

Calamus, Sweet Flag

Acorus calamus

Description: Tall, fragrant, sword-leaved plant found in marshes and borders of ponds and streams from Nova Scotia to Minnesota, southward to Florida and Texas.

Preparation: Rhizomes are collected in late autumn or spring, washed, cleaned of root fibers and dried with moderate heat. Pulverize and add to other smoking herbs.

Properties: Blackfoot used as analgesic, smoked with Tobacco for headaches (Johnston). Some contemporary references consider it psychotropic (Grubber). Smoked or smoke inhaled for colds by Omaha, Pawnee, Ponca, Winnebago, Dakota (Gilmore). Smoked for toothache by Iroquois (Herrick).

New England Aster

Aster Novae Anglia L.

Description: (See New England Aster in Smoking Flowers.)

Preparation: Pulverize root and smoke.

Properties: Chippewa smoked to attract game (Densmore).

Oshá

Ligusticum porteri

Description: "A typical parsley family plant with finely divided leaves, hollow stems, flat-topped umbels of seeds and flowers springing from a single juncture like an umbrella, and a strong celery or parsley scent. The root is large, dark brown and hairy, with a yellow, soapy inner pith and a strong, distinctive celery-butterscotch scent (Moore/Mountain)." The root system is large and spreading. The problem is in confusing this plant with the *very poisonous* Poison Hemlock. Even experts confuse them. According to Moore, half the specimens he has seen in university herbariums

that were labeled as Oshá were actually Poison Hemlock. Basically, if it is growing under 10,000 feet, presume it is Poison Hemlock. Habitat is Idaho and Nevada, Montana, Wyoming, Colorado, New Mexico, Arizona in subalpine meadows.
Preparation: Collect after seeding in September before leaves have died off. It is illegal to collect in some states as it is endangered. Collect sparingly and only if you are positive of identification. Dry roots and powder to add to smoke mixes.
Properties: The chewed root has antiviral effects. The root was traditionally added to smoke mixes for flavor, and smoked by the Cherokee for stomach problems. One of the sacred herbs of North America.

Sweet Cicely

Osmorhiza sp.
Description: Grows on lowlying, moist lands throughout United States. Large leaves with a little down underneath, lacey, triangular. It looks somewhat like Hemlock which is very poisonous.
Preparation: Use the root dried, powdered.
Properties: Pleasant aromatic anise flavor (Brounstein).

Uva Ursi, Bearberry

Arctostaphylos uva-ursi
Description: (See Bearberry in Smoking Leaves)
Preparation: Pulverize root and smoke.
Properties: Chippewa smoked to attract game (Densmore). It's interesting to note that the roots were

used to smoke before hunting game. Probably masked the human smell.

Wild Ginger

Asarum canadense, A. caudatum

Description: Natural North American habitat in North Carolina and Kansas. Blooms May-July in California, April-July in Oregon and Washington. An inconspicuous little plant, not over a foot high, found in rich soil and in woods. Usually has two heart-shaped leaves on thin hairy stems. Yellowish creeping rootstock.

Preparation: Collect root in autumn, dry and powder. Sprinkle lightly in smoke mixes. Of course, you can buy commercial ginger as root or powder as well.

Properties: Fragrant aroma, spicy and slightly bitter.

Wild Licorice

Glycyrrhiza lepidota

Description: An erect perennial that grows up to three feet tall from deep, woody rhizomes that have a licorice flavor. The leaves are alternate, each with 7-21 oblong leaflets. The flowers are yellowish-white, in spike-like clusters. Common in low spots, along riverbanks, lake shores and roadsides. Distributed from SE British Columbia across the prairies and southward into Mexico.

Preparation: Harvest roots in the autumn of mature plants before the plants have gone to seed. Use dried root powder, thoroughly mix with a light hand (Brounstein).

Properties: Flavoring.

SMOKING SEEDS

Angelica

Angelica atropurpurea

Description: (See Angelica in Smoking Roots.)

Preparation: Seeds mixed with Tobacco and used for smoking by the Delaware Indians (Tantaquidgeon). Experiment with green seeds for different flavor and strengths (Brounstein).

Properties: Angelica has many physiological effects when taken internally. When smoked as a flavoring in small amounts, it should have no system wide effects (Brounstein).

Anise

Pimpinella anisum

Description: A dainty, white-flowered, umbelliferous annual about eighteen inches high with secondary, feathery little leaves of bright green.

Preparation: Lightly sprinkle into the tobaccos to give sweet taste (Irie Herbs).

Properties: Aroma and sweetness.

Fennel

Foeniculum vulgare

Description: Tender, juicy stems and long, feathery leaves. Grows three to four feet high with an umbrella of yellow flowers.

Preparation: Gather seeds from dried stalks. Sprinkle in smoke mix.

Properties: Sweet aroma.

Prickly Poppy

Argemone sp.

Description: Prickly leaves and stems, mature height one to three feet. Flowers have five petals. "The football-shaped pods contain poppy seeds that are milky white at first, becoming mottled brown black when mature, gradually sown by the wind as the sides of the capsules curl back (Moore/Mountain)." The flowers are a luminous white that shine like miniature moons out in the brown desert.

Preparation: "[Collect] the seeds when brown and before the pod has opened, the plant when in flower. Since the sap is narcotic enough that a few moments of handling the plant results in skin insensitivity to the spines, it is necessary to gather this nasty with thick gloves. There is probably some easy way to winnow the seeds, but I have not found any, except drying the pods in the sun, covering them with burlap, and stomping them to death (Moore/Mountain)."

Properties: "[The seeds] have a sedative effect when eaten and have traditionally been smoked alone or with tobacco, but crush them a little first...they can pop in your face when lit (Moore/Desert)."

Wild Columbine

Aquilegia canadensis

Description: A perennial found in dry, rocky woods and clearings. Reaches heights of two to three feet. Charming red and yellow flowers that hang down like miniature bells. Habitat is Georgia to eastern Quebec

through New England and Ontario.
Preparation: Ripe seeds used in smoking mixture by Meskwaki (Smith).
Properties: Sweet aroma.

SMOKE FOR MEDICINAL USE ONLY

Asthma/bronchial spasms

Jimson Weed, Datura

Datura sp.
Description: A large plant with broad, spikey leaves and round stems. Beautiful, large, white, trumpetlike flowers bloom in the morning. Found in the driest, most desolate flats of the desert, along desert roads, also in foothills and drier mountains, usually forming stands in valleys and along dry washes.
Preparation: "For external use there is no advantage in collecting any one part of the plant unless it is to be used for smoking, in which case the leaves and flowers should be taken and rubbed fine after drying (Moore/Mountain)." Smoke the crushed seeds only (Brounstein). Leaves smoked by Cahuilla for asthma (Bean and Saubel).
Properties: *Datura is poisonous if taken internally!* In medicinal use as a smoke, according to Moore, "It is very useful for relaxing bronchial spasms in asthmatic attacks, the smoke from the leaves inhaled in any one of several ways....Simply sprinkling some of this dust on the flame of a cigarette lighter several times

is often sufficient. The leaves may also be rolled into a cigarette with an equal amount of the leaves from any of the wild Sages (*Salvia* sp.). An older, tried and true mixture to smoke for asthma is equal parts (in weight) of Jimson Weed, Mullein leaves, and Cubeb Berries. The effect of inhaling a puff or two of Jimson Weed is a temporary numbing of bronchial enervation which relaxes the muscles; the smoke also acts to dry up the hypersecretions of the membranes. Why this method is no longer used is beyond my understanding. Frequent use decreases its effect, but the same is true of epinephrine and isoproterenol, the drugs used in asthma inhalers. Since the function of the Jimson Weed is almost completely local, there is no need to inhale enough to get into the bloodstream; the others all have strong systemic effects and can cause a rebound in some individuals, as well as a whole host of adverse reactions. For sinus inflammations a little smoke inhaled through the nostrils will bring some temporary relief to the swollen mucosa (Moore/Mountain)." Used as a sacred plant in many indigenous cultures.

TOBACCO FOR CEREMONIAL USE

Punche, Wild Tobacco

Nicotiana attenuata
Dzil Nat'oh, Mountain Smoke (Navajo)
Description: Annual plant, one to three feet tall covered with gland-type hairs that are sticky. The leaves

are narrow and tapered, up to six inches long. Found at 1,000 to 7,5000 feet (Boone). Native species found from California to west Texas and north to Colorado, Utah and Nevada, most frequently in meadows, flats, flood plains, dry streams and desert from sea level to 7,000 feet.

Preparation: Tobacco must be cured to be smokable.

Properties: Used as a ritual offering to Spirit either as dried leaf or as smoke throughout North American First Nations, Central and South America.

Tree Tobacco

Nicotiana glauca Graham

Nat'oh tsoh, Big Smoke (Navajo)

Description: Dark green shrubs or small trees with oval to oblong leaves. Found in sandy areas often near water up to 5,000 feet (Boone).

Preparation: Tobacco must be cured to be smokable.

Properties: Used as ritual offering to Spirit by all North American First Nations, as well as in Central and South America. Used in the Navajo Blessing Way. Used to replenish good spirits in one's body (Boone).

Sumach (*Rhus glabra*)

Smoke Plants of North America

All of these plants have some documented use as a plant to be smoked in a pipe. (There are many more plants which are burned in the environment—smudged—and the smoke inhaled for medicinal or ceremonial purposes.) I have included the part of the plant to be smoked and its use when it was available. For many of the Navajo plants, I have only the name.

Most of the Navajo plant names come from Joseph Winter's list of Navajo smoke plants in *Tobacco Use by Native North Americans, Sacred Smoke and Silent Killer*. Most of the other references to Native American usage come from Dan Moerman's *Native American Ethnobotany Database*. Those that are marked have more detailed information in the previous section. Some of these plants I've smoked, and many of them I haven't. Some plants with historical usage may not be safe to smoke without expert knowledge.

Alumroot
Heuchera parvifolia
Navajo Canyon Rat's Tobacco, Sparkling (Spotted) Wind's Tobacco

~American Angelica, Great Purple Angelica (roots, seeds)
Angelica atropurpurea

~Anise (seeds)
Pimpinella anisum

Aspen
Populous tremuloides aurea
Hopi smoking mixture

~Aster (roots)
Aster puniceus

Aster
Aster oblongifolius
Navajo Sheep Tobacco

Avens
Geum sp.

Bastard Toadflax
Comondra pallida
Navajo Slim Beetle's Tobacco

Bayberry (plant)
Myrica cerifera
Seminole

~Bearberry, Uva-Ursi (leaves, root)
Arctostaphylos uva-ursi

Beardtongue
Penstemon neomexicanus, P. palmeri
Navajo Sheep Tobacco, Talking God's Tobacco

Bee Plant
Cleome lutea
NavajoYellow Bee Weed

~Bent Grass (leaves)
Agrostis palustris Huds
Navajo Sun Smoke

Bergamot, Horsemint
Monarda pectinata
Navajo Jagged Medicine

~Betony, Lousewort, Elephant's Head, Parrot's Beak, Indian Warrior (flowers)
Pedicularis sp.

Biscuit Root, California Rock Parsnip (roots)
Lomatium dissectum, L. californicum
Paiute, Karok

~Blackberry (leaves, root)
Rubus sp.

Blazingstar
Mentzelia pumila
Navajo Slender or Big Tenacious

Blueberry, Whortleberry (leaves)
Vaccinium angustifolum
Okanagon, Gosiute

Cryptantha jamesii
Navajo Racer's Tobacco

Broadbean (leaves)
Vicia faba
Navajo

Brickellbush
Brickellia oblongifolia var. *linifolila*
Navajo Bat's Tobacco, Thin Tobacco

Bristly Crowfoot
Ranunculus pensylvanicus

Brittle Bush, Incensio
Encilia farinosa Gray
Navajo Tobacco in Blessing Way ceremony

Buckbean, Bog Bean (leaves)
Menyanthes trijoliata

Buckbrush (leaves)
Ceanothus sp.
Paiute

Bur Sage
Ambrosia tenuifolia Spreng

Butterweed, Horse-weed, Fleabane
(dried flowers)
Erigeron canadensis, E. philadelphicus
Ojibwa

~Calamus, Sweet Flag (root)
Acorus calamus

Catchfly, Campion
Silene douglasii
Navajo, part of the Bead Chant Tobacco and Coyote Tobacco; Gosiute

Carrot
Daucus carota
Navajo Big Pleiades Tobacco

Catnip (leaves)
Nepeta cataria
Shinnecock

Chickweed, Starwort
Stellaria jamesiana
Navajo Big Dipper's Tobacco

Cinquefoil
Potentilla sp.

~Coltsfoot (leaves)
Tussilago farfara

Corydalis
Corydalis aurea
Navajo Raven's Tobacco

Corn Silk
Zea mays

Cottonwood (inner bark, leaf galls)
Populus angustifolia, P. balsamifera
Inuktitut, Montana Indian

Crinkled Toothwort (leaves)
Cardamine diphylla
Cherokee

~Damiana (leaves)
Turnera diffusa

~Deer's Tongue, Wild Vanilla (leaves)
Liatris odoratissima

Devil's Club, Devil's Walking Stick (root)
Oplopanax horridum
Cheyenne, Crow for headaches

Desert Rue (dried stems)
Thamnosma montana
Shoshoni for colds

~Dittany (leaves)
Cunila origanoides

Divergent Wild Buckwheat
Eriogonum divaricatum
Kayenta Navajo for snake bite

Dock
Rumex fueginus
Navajo Sky Tobacco

Dogbane, Indian Hemp
Apocynum suksdorfii var. angustifolium
Navajo Green Frog Tobacco

~Dogwood, Red Osier Dogwood,
Red Willow (bark)
Cornus sp.

Elkweed (leaves)
Frasera speciosa
Ramah Navaho for healing the mind

Evening Primrose (plant)
Oenothera multijuga, O. scapoidea
Navajo Lizard's Tobacco, Hopi

Eyebright (leaves)
Euphrasia officinalis

Fendlerbush
Fendlera rupicola
Navajo Talking God's Tobacco

~Fennel (seeds)
Foeniculum vulgare

Four O'clock (leaves)
Mirabilis oxybaphoides
Navajo Snake Tobacco, part of Beadway Tobacco

Giant Trumpets
Macrome ria viridiflora
Hopi for healing the mind

Gilia, Starflower
Gilia longifolia
Navajo Eagle Tobacco, Blessingway Tobacco

Ginseng, American (leaves, dried roots)
Panax quinquefolius
Iroquois

Globemallow (top of plant)
Sphaeralcea coccinea
Navajo Whirling Coyote Tobacco

~Golden Eye (Sunflower Compositae)
Viguiera sp.

.

~Goldenrod (flowers)
Solidago graminifolla, S. canadensis
Navajo Blue Lizard Tobacco

Gray Birch (bark)
Betulaceae sp.

Groundsel
Senecio neomexicanus
Navajo Born for Water's Tobacco

Groundsel tree
Baccharis glutinosa
NavajoWaterway Lotion, Excessway Tobacco

Hawthorne (bark)
Crataegus sp.
Ojibwa for hunting

~Hops (strobiles)
Humulus americanus

Horehound (leaves)
Marrubium vulgare

Indian Paint Brush
Castilleja minor (C. affinis)
Navajo Smelly Tobacco

Indian Turnip (leaves)
Psoralidum tenuiflorum
Navajo Night Chant Tobacco

Indigo Bush
Parosela lanata
Navajo Centipede's Tobacco

~Jimson Weed, Datura (leaves, flowers, seeds)
Datura sp.

Juniper, "Cedar" (leaves)
Juniperus monosperma and others

Lavender (flowers)
Lavandula sp.

Lead Plant (leaves)
Amorpha canescens
Oglala

Lemon Balm (leaves)
Melissa officinalis

Life Everlasting (leaves)
Gnaphalium polycephalum

~Lobelia, Red Lobelia, Indian Tobacco (leaves)
Lobelia inflata, L. cardinalis

Locoweed
Oxytropis lambertii
Navajo Odiferous Crow's Tobacco, Sheep Tobacco, Bighorn Tobacco

Lovage (root)
Lingusticum canadense
Cherokee for stomach, Cowasuck for flavoring

Madrona (leaves)
Arbutus menziesii
Hoh, Quileute

Maidenhair Fern, Avenca
Adiantum sp.
Kayenta Navajo smoked for healing the mind.

~Manzanita (leaves)
Arctostaphylos sp.

Meadowsweet
Spiraea alba

Milkvetch, Vetch
Astragalus lonchocarpus,
Navajo Brown Crane's Tobacco

Milkvetch, Vetch
A. scaposus (A. calycosus)

~Mint (leaves)
Mentha

Mohave Sandwort (root, leaves)
Arenaria macradenia
Kawaiisu (root) for sinus, headaches; Shoshoni (leaves) for smoke mix

~Mullein (leaves, flowers)
Verbascum Thapsus L.
Navajo Deer Ears

Musquash (root)
Cicuta maculata
Ojibwa for hunting

~Nettle, Stinging Nettle (leaves)
Urtica dioca

~New England Aster (flowers, root)
Aster Novae Anglia L.

Noble Fir, Balsam Fir (leaves)
Pinaceae sp.
Paiute and Ojibwa for colds

Onosmodium thurberi
Hopi "Sacred Tobacco" to bring rain

~Oshá (root)
Ligusticum porteri

Paperflower
Psilostrophe sparsifolia
Navajo Stick Medicine, Owl's Feet

Partridgeberry, Squaw Vine
Mitchella repens

~Passionflower (flower)
Passiflora mexicana, P. foetida, P tenuiloba, P. incarnata

~Pearly Everlasting (leaves)
Anaphalis margaritacea

~Pipsissewa and Pyrola (leaves)
Chimaphila sp. and *Pyrola* sp.

Pigweed
Amaranthus groecizans (A. albus)
Navajo, the ones that lie spreading (*A. blitoides*), heaped grass (*A. retroflexus*)

Plantain
Plantago
Navajo for ceremonial use

Ponderosa Pine
Pinus ponderosa
Hopi smoke mix for ceremonial purposes

Prairie Smoke (scraped root)
Geumtriflorum
Blackfoot for clearing the head

Prickly Ash (bark)
Zanthoxylum americanum
Iroquois for toothaches

~Prickly Poppy (seeds)
Argemone sp.

Purple Meadow Rue (seeds)
Thalictrum dasycarpum
Potawatomi for hunting and love medicine

Puncture Vine
Tribulus terrestris (maximus)
Navajo Bear Tobacco, part of Bead Chant Tobacco

Purslane
Portlaca retusa
Navajo Fringed Basket

~Pussytoes, Pink Pussytoes (leaves)
Antennaria neglecta, A. aprica, A. rosea Greene
Navajo Coyote Bed

Rabbit Brush
Chrysothamnus sp.
Navajo, a Tobacco in Evilway prayer sticks

~Raspberry (leaves)
Rubus sp.

Red Alder (leaves)
Alnus rubra
Makah

Rose (leaves)
Rosa gymnocarpa
Okanagon

Rosemary (leaves)
Rosmarinus officinalis

~Sage, White Sage, Black Sage, Purple Sage, Garden Sage (leaves)
Salvia dorii, S. carnosa Dougl
Navajo Prayer Smoke, Beautiful Smoke, Gray Tobacco

~Sagebrush, Mugwort, Wormwood (leaves)
Artemisia sp.
Corn Tobacco

Salal (leaves)
Gaultheria shallon
Makah

~Sassafras (bark)
Sassafras albidum

~Scotch Broom, Spanish Broom (flowers)
Cytisus scoparius, Spartium junceum

Self-Heal (leaves)
Prunella vulgaris

Skeleton Plant
Lygodesmia rostrata
Navajo Antelope Tobacco, Alarmed Navajo Tobacco

~Skullcap (leaves)
Scutellaria sp.

Scurfpea
Psoralea tenuiflora
Navajo Tobacco, Beeweed

Slippery Elm (leaves)
Ulmus rubra
Iroquois for catarrh

~Spicebush (leaves)
Lindera benzoin

Spikenard (roots)
Aralia racemosa
Malecite mixed with Red Osier Dogwood for headaches

Spreading Dogbane (leaves)
Apocynum androsaemifolium
Okanagan-Colville for aphrodisiac

~Strawberry (leaves)
Frugaria sp.

Sunflower
Helianthus sp.
Navajo Sun's Tobacco

~ Sweet Cicely (root)
Osmorhiza sp.

~Sweet Clover (flowers)
Melilotus officinalis M. alba

~Sumach, Smooth Sumach, Staghorn Sumach (leaves, berries)
Rhus glabra, *R. typhina*

~Sweet Grass (leaves)
Hierochloe odorata

~Sweet Gum (leaves)
Liquidambar styraciflua

Tansy (flowers)
Tanacetum vulgare
Ojibwa for deer hunting

Thyme (leaves)
Thymus serphyllum

~Tobacco, Wild Tobacco, Punche (leaves)
Nicotiana sp.
Navajo *Dzil Nat'oh*, Mountain Smoke

~Tree Tobacco (leaves)
Nicotiana glauca Graham
Navajo Nat'oh tsoh, Big Smoke

Umbrella Plant
Eriogonum alatum, E. divaricatum, E. jamesii
Navajo Earth Medicine, Knotted Medicine, Resembling Big Snake's Horns, Yellow Flower with Tobacco, Mountain Tobacco

Valerian (leaves)
Valeriana sitchensis
Okanagon

Venus Looking Glass
Tridonis perfoliata
Meskwaki for ceremonies

Vetch
Vicia americana
Navajo Water Tobacco

Violet (leaves, flowers)
Viola odorata

Waterleaf (leaves)
Hydrophyllum sp.

White Tumbleweed
Amaranthus albus
Navajo for Coyote Chant

Wild Asparagus
Shinnersoseris rostrata (Gray) S. Tom
Navajo as sedative

~Wild Columbine (seeds)
Aquilegia canadensis

~Wild Ginger (root)
Asarum canadense, A. caudatum

Wild Lettuce (sap)
Lactuca virosa

~Wild Licorice (root)
Glycyrrhiza lepidota

Wild Rose (inner bark)
Rosa arkansana var. *suffulta*
Pawnee, Omaha, Dakota

~Willow (bark)
Salix sp.

Willowweed, Willow Herb
Epilobium angustifolium
Navajo Red Blackbird's Tobacco

Winterfat
Eurotia sp.?
Navajo Jackrabbit Food

~Yarrow (leaves, flowers)
Achillea millefolium

Yellow Pimpernel (seeds)
Taenidia integerrima
Ojibwa for hunting

Yerba Buena (leaves)
Satureja douglasii

~Yerba Santa (leaves)
Eriodictyon sp.

Yew (needles)
Taxus brevifolia
Clallum

Notes

1. There's a growing awareness that elements besides the Tobacco plant may be the carcinogenic trigger, especially additives, pesticides, and herbicides. It is known that the pesticides and herbicides used on Tobacco, when burned, become even more toxic. A lesser known danger is contamination with the fungus aflatoxin, which also contaminates peanuts and corn.

Aflatoxin, a toxic metabolite produced by the common fungus Aspergillus, is a problem when commodities are stored in damp and warm environments. Aflatoxin contamination in cigarettes [and marijuana] may be an extreme health danger. Aflatoxin worsens the carcinogenic effects of Tobacco consumption. The level and extent of aflatoxin contamination is *not* being monitored in Tobacco products...there is a complete disregard for monitoring the presence of this fungal toxin in tobacco products and it is one of the most potent carcinogens known. In addition...Aflatoxin causes mutations in the p 54 tumor-suppressor gene at codon 249 in liver cells, the same site often mutated in lung cancer. It is highly unlikely that this is a coincidence. News Release July 12, 2002 **www.tobacco.org**

2. "The advent of the cigarette-rolling machine in the 1880s marked the beginning of the end to the rarity of pulmonary carcinoma...As early as 1941,

Ochsner and DeBakey noted the striking similarity of the curves for cigarette sales and for primary cancer of the lungs. Sales of pipe tobacco and of cigars in the past never approached such a strong association…Though the degree of inhalation is undoubtedly important, it is unlikely that 'all types of tobacco smoke (regardless of source)' are equally dangerous. For reasons not yet elucidated, cigarette smoke is much the greater culprit." Larry Kirkland, letter to the Editor. *JAMA, The Journal of the American Medical Association*, Feb. 26, 1992, v267 n8 p1073(2).

Several studies throughout the twentieth century have documented the low incidence of cancer, including lung cancer, among Native Americans.

"In 1926, F. L. Hoffman surveyed physicians who provided health care to approximately 100,000 Native Americans and identified only 276 cancer deaths in total and not one lung cancer death (Samet: 335)." Lung cancer and other chronic diseases of smoking remain relatively uncommon among Native Americans in the United States, especially among the southwestern tribes, though some evidence indicates this may be changing with increased use of commercial cigarettes. There is not enough data to document the health effects of ritual smoking in the past. Jonathan Samet. "Health Effects of Tobacco Use by Native Americans, Past and Present." In *Tobacco Use by Native North*

Americans, Sacred Smoke and Silent Killer, edited by Joseph Winter, pp. 336-341.

3. "Xanax is a drug prescribed for anxiety and stress. It is the most prescribed drug in America. It is habit-forming and addictive. Its "anti-anxiety" effect is an early stage of central nervous system depression, similar to the chemical effect of alcohol and barbiturates. Withdrawal can cause life-threatening neurological reactions, fever, psychosis, seizure, lowered blood pressure, severe cramps, loss of memory, disorientation, anxiety, panic, and insomnia. People taking one Xanax a day for a few weeks can become addicted. It takes the brain 6-18 months to recover from the effects of Xanax." Peter Breggin, M.D., excerpt from *Toxic Psychiatry* on the Web citing John Steinberg, Medical Director of Chemical Dependency, Program of Greater Baltimore Medical Center, President of Maryland Society of Addiction Medicine.

4. The National Institute of Health estimates that 80% of all ailments are linked to chronic stress.

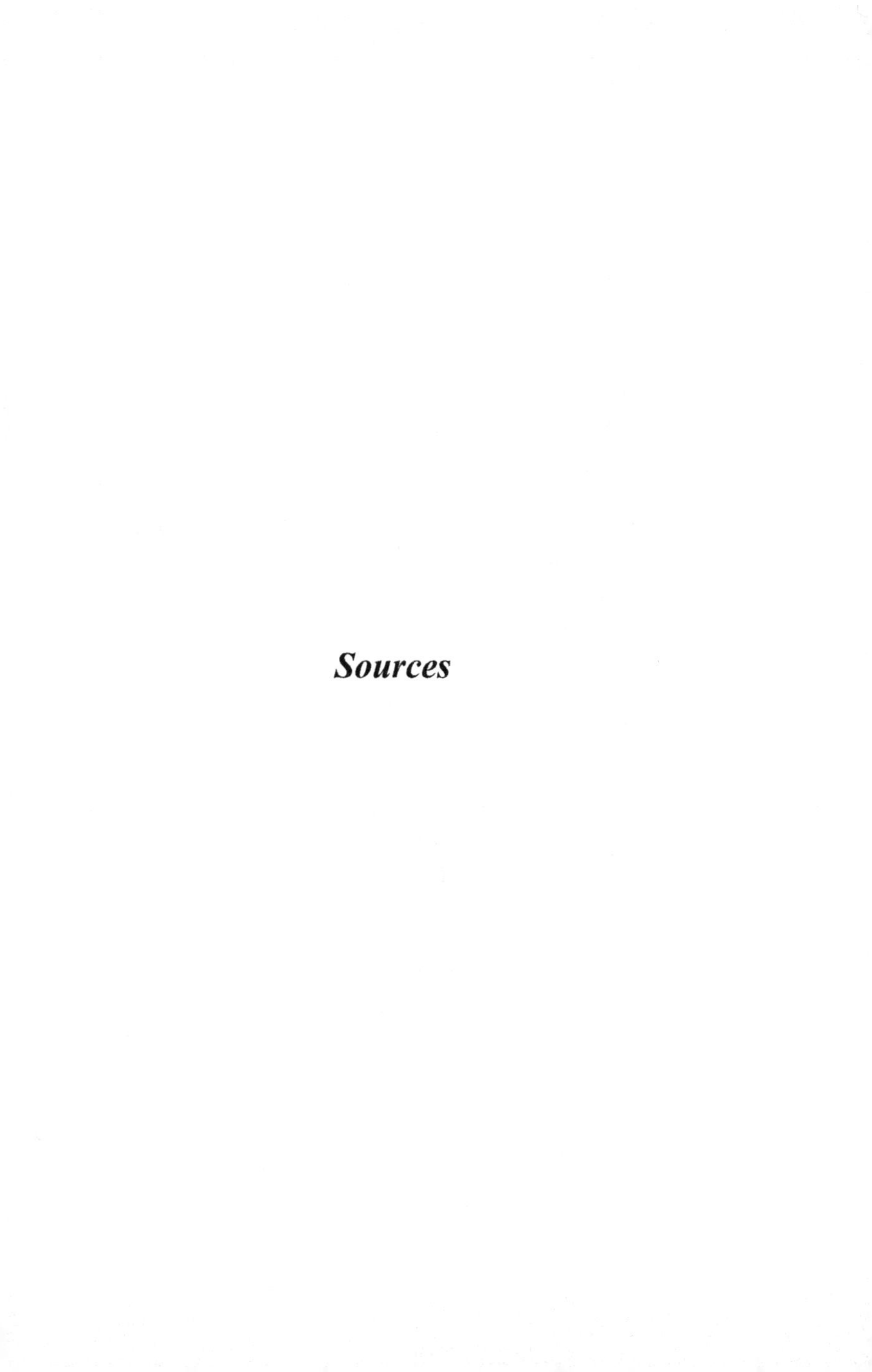

Sources

BOOKS

Adams, Karen and Mollie Toll. "Tobacco Use, Ecology, and Manipulation in the Prehistoric and Historic Southwestern United States." In *Tobacco Use by Native North Americans, Sacred Smoke and Silent Killer* edited by Joseph Winter.

Awiakta, Marilu. *Selu, Seeking the Corn Mother's Wisdom* (Golden, CO: Fulcrum Publishing, 1994). I found this book in Tahlequah, Cherokee Nation, and was drawn to it because Awiakta's family comes from the same part of Tennessee as my family. Very much worth reading for her perspective on the sacred message of Corn, plants, relationships, and life. Awiakta also has an interesting essay about Barbara McClintock who won the Nobel Prize for her work with corn genetics. See Evelyn Keller Fox, *A Feeling for the Organism: The Life and Work of Barbara McClintock* (New York: W.H. Freeman, 1983).

Beaumier, J.P. and L. Camp. *The Pipe Smoker* (New York: Harper & Row, 1980). The authors make the distinction between cigarette and pipe smoking. The book was written under pseudonyms of two psychologists and I believe one works for a pipe manufacturing company.

Buhner, Stephen Harrod. *Sacred and Herbal Healing Beers: The Secrets of Ancient Fermentation* (Boulder, CO: Siris Books, an imprint of Brewers Publications, 1998).
Buhner has written the most fascinating, definitive and soul-expanding book on fermention of plants and its sacred relationship with humans. His understanding of the consequences of banishing the sacred use of plants to the shadow is almost identical to mine. A must read, as are his other books on sacredness and plants.

Cowan, Eliot. *Plant Spirit Medicine: The Healing Power of Plants* (Newberg, OR: Swan Raven & Co., 1999).

Densmore, Frances. *How Indians Use Wild Plants (For Food, Medicine and Crafts)* formerly titled *Uses of Plants by Chippewa Indians* (New York: Dover Publications, 1974). Densmore's work was originally published in the Forty-fourth Annual Report of the Annual Report of the Bureau of American Ethnology 1926-1927. The sections of this report which are Densmore's are pages 275-397. The author's interaction with the Chippewa seemed to be quite in depth and her report includes the daily details of activities that are so hard to come by.

Louis-Philippe, King of France, trans., by Stephen Becker. *Diary of My Travels in America* (New York:

Delacorte Press, 1977). I ran across a couple of interesting comments from this diary about smoke plants which were quoted on the Web.

Lowie, Robert H. *The Crow Indians* (New York: Farrar & Rinehart, Inc, 1935).

Marriott, Alice. *The Ten Grandmothers* (Norman, OK: University of Oklahoma Press, 1945). This book was given to me by my Sauk and Fox/Quapaw friend in Tahlequah. Marriott was an anthropologist who collected stories from Kiowas who lived through the transition from their traditional way of life to reservation and rewrote them in narrative style. The Kiowa perspective on power I found quite fascinating: i.e., not everyone "gets" power even if they go looking for it, and those who do get power have a responsibility to the power and to their people in the use of that power.

Mayes, Vernon and Barbara Lacey Bayless. *Nanisé, A Navajo Herbal: One Hundred Plants from the Navajo Reservation* (Tsaile, AZ: Navajo Community College Press, 1989). A beautiful, informative book with wonderful botanical illustrations.

McClintock, Walter. *The Old North Trail or Life, Legends and Religion of the Blackfeet* (Lincoln & London: University of Nebraska, 1910).

Moore, Michael. *Medicinal Plants of the Desert and Canyon West* (Santa Fe, NM: Museum of New Mexico Press, 1984).

Medicinal Plants of the Mountain West (Santa Fe, NM: Museum of New Mexico Press, 1979). There are very few books on wild plants that give an interested lay person enough information to actually go out on their own and find and use plants medicinally. Moore's knowledge comes from hands-on experience as a clinician, plant gatherer, merchant, teacher, and plant lover. Moore includes more useful information in one paragraph about a specific plant than others do in a whole chapter. Plus, he has a wicked sense of humor and does not pander to the growing "fear of wild plants" phenomenon. His Web site provides extensive and free access to his encyclopedic knowledge. Follow the links on his sources list for reputable herbs dealers.

Neihardt, John G. *Black Elk Speaks* (Lincoln and London: University of Nebraska Press, 1998). A classic in Native American literature. Black Elk (Lakota) shared with Neihardt his visions and philosophy. More recent editions have a notes section in the back that compares Neihardt's text with the stenographic notes of what Black Elk literally said. There are some important differences.

Paper, Jordan. *The Sacred Pipe and Native American Religion* (Moscow, ID: University of Idaho Press, 1988). An in-depth study focusing primarily on the pipe as the central aspect of the ritual ceremonial use of smoking. More recent studies focus on tobacco and plants as the primary sacred material. Well written and interesting. Good bibliography.

von Gernet, Alexander. "North American Indigenous Nicotiana Use and Tobacco Shamanism, The Early Documentary Record, 1520-1660." In *Tobacco Use by Native North Americans, Sacred Smoke and Silent Killer* edited by Joseph Winter.

Weed, Susun. All of Susun Weed's books on plants and herbalism are wonderful. She knows *all* about Nettles.

Winter, Joseph C. ed., *Tobacco Use by Native North Americans, Sacred Smoke and Silent Killer* (Norman, OK: University of Oklahoma Press, 2000).
The most authoritative and fascinating publication on *Nicotiana* to date. Although Winter does make the point that "tobacco" may or may not be *Nicotiana,* almost all of the book is about the *Nicotiana* type of Tobacco. However, he includes a rare and valuable list of non-*Nicotiana* plants smoked by the Navajo—the most extensive list I've found, even

though there is no information on preparation and usage. Winter heads the Native American Plants Cooperative which grows and distributes ceremonial Tobacco to Native Americans.

JOURNALS

Boone, Sam B., Jill Dedera, Phyllis Hogan."Plants–Nanisé (Living Things)," *Official Journal of the Arizona Ethnobotanical Research Association*, Vol. One, No. 2, Summer Solstice, 1988. Reprint Series 2000.

Jackson, Jerome, Erin Humphreys, Phyllis Hogan. "Interview with Jerome Jackson, Navajo Plant Gatherer," *Official Journal of the Arizona Ethnobotanical Research Association*, Vol. Two, No. 1, Fall Equinox, 2000.
I discovered this gem of a journal when I attended the annual conference of the Arizona Ethnobotanical Research Association in Flagstaff, Arizona. The interviews with Sam B. Boone, Navajo Herbalist, and Jerome Jackson, Navajo Plant Gatherer, are rare first-hand accounts of the use of medicinal plants from the Navajo perspective.

Cohen, Ken. "Native American Medicine," *Alternative Therapies in Health and Medicine*, Aliso Viejo, Nov 1998. Vol. 4, Issue 6, start page 45.
I met Ken Cohen at a conference in Winslow,

Arizona which had the theme of integrating Western and Native American medicine modalities. He was teaching a Qigong class. Cohen studied with a Cherokee Medicine Elder for years and has a vast knowledge of many traditions of medicine.

Everett, Erin. "Indigenous Medicine for Modern Humans, An Interview with Eliot Cowan," *New Life Journal*, Oct/Nov 2001.

Murie, James. "Pawnee Indian Societies," *Anthropological papers of the American Museum of Natural History*, 1914:561-567.

COMMERCIAL FLYERS

Irie Herbs, *Traditional Diné Healing Herbs For The Healing of the Nations*, c/o Cimi Boone, 31 Leupp Road, Flagstaff, AZ 86004.
I obtained this extraordinarily informative flyer about Navajo herbs at the same conference in Winslow, Arizona, where I met Ken Cohen. It was at a table set up with many jars of Navajo/Diné smoking and medicinal herbs. Later, I contacted Cimi and purchased some Navajo pipes from her made by her uncle. The Irie Herbs flyer is where I first learned the Navajo use of tobaccos to heal and strengthen the mind, supporting my personal experience.

Winter Sun Trading Company, *Plants of the Winter Sun*, c/o Phyllis Hogan, 107 N. San Francisco Suite #1, Flagstaff, AZ 86001. 928-774-2884.
Phyllis Hogan is one of the extraordinary herbalists of our generation. She is also the director of the Arizona Ethnobotanical Research Association and editor of its journal. Her flyer is a lesson in herbalism and has interesting smoke mixes.

WEB

ASH. A comprehensive web site with information on commercial tobacco.
www.ash.org.
A good fact sheet on how commercial tobacco cultivation affects the environment is at www.ash.org.uk/html/fact22.html.

Breggin, Peter. *Toxic Psychiatry.*
*www.*breggin.com/minortranqs.html
Excerpts from the book online. Will make you think about your choice of medicine to reduce stress, anxiety and depression.

Brounstein, Howie. *Herbal Smoking Mixtures.*
www.teleport.com
Brounstein is a knowledgable herbalist and wildcrafter. His informative book on smoking herbs, available on the Web or for purchase in hard copy, is the most authoritative contemporary document

available. It was very reassuring to me when I started down this path. You can find out about his herbal school and field trips to gather wild plants at his Web site. He has good guidelines for wildcrafting as well.

Chamberlin, Ralph. *Ethnobotany of the Gosiute Indians of Utah.*
Southwest School of Botanical Medicine Homepage
www.chili.rt66.com/hrbmoore/HOMEPAGE/
HomePage.html

Cimino, E., A. Sayers, R. Roods. *The Sacred Use of Tobacco.* Costanoan Ohlone Indian Canyon Resource.
www.udayton.edu/~health/syllabi/tobacco/
native04.htm

Cowasuck Band of the Pennacook-Abenaki People, The People of the White Pines. *Smoking and Pipes.*
www.cowasuck.org.
Excellent web site with information on traditional smoking, pipes, and herbs.

Grieve, Maude. *A Modern Herbal.*
www.botanical.com
A classic of Western herbalism is on the Web.

Grubber, Hudson. *Growing the Hallucinogens.*
www.erowid.org/psychoactives

Good, solid information on growing plants, many of which *I* would not classify as "hallucinogens." As the governmental controls on herbs tighten, and the commercialization of herbs erodes their quality, growing your own may be the best way to obtain the herbs you want.

Hickey, Ellen and Yenyen Chan. *Tobacco, Farmers and Pesticides: The Other Story.*
www.igc.org/panna/resources/documents/tobacco.dv.html
Extremely well-researched and well-written report on commercial Tobacco, worker, farmer, and pesticide abuse.

Indian Country. *Ceremonial Use of Tobacco.*
www.mpm.edu/wirp/ICW-166.html

Johnstone, Paula. *The Selfless Spirit of Tobacco Medicine.*
Use search engine.

Moore, Michael. Southwest School of Botanical Medicine
www.swsbm.com
One of the master herbalists of our times. His Web site is one of the marvels of the modern world. Bored? Check out the Ethnobotany Manuals and the distribution maps of 294 herbs.

Native American Ethnobotany Database
www.umd.umich.edu/cgi-bin/herb
Dan Moerman spent twenty-five years putting this database together. You can access it on the Web at the above URL or in book form (*Native American Botany*, Portland, OR: Timber Press, 1998). Over fifty of the plants in this book are from his database. I used the key words: smoke, smoke plant, smoking, and smoked. If you want to follow all the smoke plants on the list to their source, this is one place to start. The following references are from this database:

Bean, Lowell John and Katherine Siva Saubel. *Temalpakh (From the Earth)—Cahuilla Indian Knowledge and Usage of Plants* (Banning, CA: Malki Museum Press, 1972).

Chestnut, V. K. *Plants used by the Indians of Mendocino County, Calif.* Contributions from the U.S. National Herbarium 7:295-408 (371), 1902.

Gilmore, Melvin R. *Uses of Plants by the Indians of the Missouri River Region.* SI-BAE Annual Report #33, 1919.

Goodrich, Jennie and Claudia Lawson. *Kashaya Pomo Plants.* (Los Angeles: American Studies Center, University of California Los Angeles, 1980).

Fewkes, J. Walter. "A Contribution to Ethno-botany," *American Anthropologist* 9:14-21, 1896

Grinnell, George Bird. *The Cheyenne Indians—Their History and Ways of Life* Vol. 2 (Lincoln, NE: University of Nebraska Press, 1972).

Hamel, Paul B. and Mary U. Chiltoskey. *Cherokee Plants and Their Uses—A 400 Year History* (Sylva, NC: Herald Publishing Co., 1975).

Herrick, James William. *Iroquois Medical Botany* (Albany, NY: State University of New York, Ph.D. Thesis, 1977).

Hocking, George M. *Some Plant Materials Used Medicinally and Otherwise by the Navajo Indians in the Chaco Canyon, New Mexico* (El Palacio 56:146-165, 1956).

Johnston, Alex. *Plants and the Blackfoot* (Lethbridge, Alberta: Lethbridge Historical Society, 1987).

Smith, Huron H. *Ethnobotany of the Meskwaki Indians* (Bulletin of the Public Museum of the City of Milwaukee 4:175-326, 1928).

Tantaquidgeon, Gladys. *A Study of Delaware Indian Medicine Practice and Folk Beliefs* (Harrisburg, Pennsylvania Historical Commission, 1942).

Vestal, Paul A. *The Ethnobotany of the Ramah Navajo* (Papers of the Peabody Museum of American Archaeology and Ethnology 40 (4):1-94).

Whiting, Alfred F. *Ethnobotany of the Hopi* (Museum of Northern Arizona Bulletin #15, 1939).

ORGANIZATIONS

A portion of the profits from this book will be donated to the following organizations, as well as to individuals who are preserving valuable plant knowledge.

Arizona Ethnobotanical Research Association
Director, Phyllis Hogan
107 N. San Francisco, Suite #1
Flagstaff, AZ 86001
928-774-2884
Publishes the *Official Journal of the Arizona Ethnobotanical Research Association.* Refreshingly authentic research untainted by tenure and academic politics. If you can, make it to one of their annual conferences. Amazingly interesting people. Open membership.

Native American Plant Cooperative
Director, Joseph Winter
P.O. Box 36749
Albuquerque, NM 87176
505-277-5853
Grows native Tobacco and accepts donations of Tobacco and other smoking herbs for Native American ceremonial use, especially for incarcerated Native Americans. Has an education program about the difference between commercial and ceremonial Tobacco.

Native Seeds/SEARCH
526 N. 4th Ave.
Tucson, AZ 85705
520-622-5561
This organization was founded in 1983 as a result of requests from Native Americans in southern Arizona who wanted to grow traditional crops but no longer had the traditional seeds. It has become a major regional seed bank, a unique resource for traditional and modern agriculture. It includes 1800 collections, more than 90% of which are not being preserved anywhere else. They are providing an incredibly valuable service to preserve our genetic seed heritage. Membership is open to everyone. Membership and seeds are free to Native Americans living in the greater Southwest.

Hops (*Humulus americanus*)

PLANT AND PIPE SOURCES

These are some sources that I have used. For others, go to Michael Moore's Web site. Mass-produced and processed herbs are *not* the same as ethically wild-crafted or organically grown. When I sat in on Michael's class on Passionflower, he described the commercial process of drying this delicate herb in huge, hot dryers. You think there's going to be much juju left after that? No way. Grow your own or purchase from people who care about *plants.*

Horizon Herbs, Strictly Medicinal Seeds
Featuring Organically Grown and
Wild-Harvested Seed
Organically Grown Live Roots and Plants
PO Box 69, Williams, OR 97544-0069
541-846-6704
www.horizonherbs.com
hhcustserv@horizonherbs.com
Their catalog is fabulous. I was up all night reading it.

Two Ravens Herbals,
LLC. Rt.1, Box 172, Kooskia, Idaho 83539
208-926-7833
www.tworavensherbals.com.
tworavens@cybrquest.com
Two graduates of Michael Moore's school. Wonderful herbs with great vibes.

In Harmony Herbs & Spices
www.inharmonyherbs.com
1862 1/2 Bacon St., San Diego, CA 92107
619-223-8051
They sell small quantities of lovely herbs.

Jim McDonald, Herbalist
www.herbcraft.org
A great place to learn more about herbs.

Pacific Botanicals, LLC
4350 Fish Hatchery Road, Grants Pass, OR 97527
541-479-7777
Yummy, yummy, yummy herbs in bulk. Try the commercial Hops, try theirs. Not even on the same planet. Oh, go ahead and order a whole pound!

Sky Dancer Pipes
www.arizonarts.com
928-593-0336
skydancer545@yahoo.com
So many people have asked where to buy a good pipe. Frances and Steve at Sky Dancer hand carve beautiful traditional and functional pipes from catlinite pipe stone and sell them reasonably.

Winter Sun Trading Company
(also see Commercial Flyers)
www.wintersun.com
Great smoke mixes and herbal wisdom.

To Contact:

MultiCultural Educational
Publishing Company
POB 1054, Jerome, AZ 86331

Phone: 928-649-5449
Email: orders@mcepub.com

Book Order Form

Postal Orders: MultiCultural Educational
Publishing Company
POB 1054, Jerome, AZ 86331

___ Check ___ Money Order

Please send me:

________ (Qty)	***Smoke Plants of North America*** at $15.95 each
________	Subtotal
________	Sales Tax (Arizona addresses - add 9.2%)
________	Shipping (1st book $4.00. Additional books $2.00 each)
________	International shipping (1st book $9.00. Additional books $5.00 each, estimated)
________	TOTAL

Name ____________________________

Address ____________________________

City ____________________________

State, Zip ____________________________

Telephone ____________________________

Email ____________________________

Made in the USA
Las Vegas, NV
17 May 2024

90014377R00115